In her flowing  Nesbitt helps us to view our wilderness seasons—and all of life—through Heaven's eyes. In the midst of difficulty, your hope will be restored and your perspective lifted as you soak in this biblical revelation of God's fathomless love.

Cathy Larson
RadiusNetwork.org

If you need a clearer understanding of how God is working in the challenging seasons of your life, read this book. Tiffany vulnerably weaves together her personal journey with solid biblical truths, enabling you to catch a glimpse of how God is crafting your own unique story. The end result is a fresh outpouring of joy and strength to endure!

Sally Cook
Author, Speaker and Co-Founder of Hope Refuge

In *Into the Wilderness*, Tiffany Nesbitt takes her readers on a deep dive—both theologically into the biblical text and personally into her own journey through wilderness seasons, exploring life's most painful questions: Did I miss you, God? Did you fail me, God? At the same time, she boldly addresses the contemporary syncretism of 'a pinch of Jesus, a cupful of humanism and a strong dash of follow-your-heart ideology' as a deceptive trap leading to greater bondage. While artfully unmasking the world's self-absorbed ideal of 'standing taller' in times of suffering as a counterfeit solution, she urges us to 'lean lower' into our Beloved. Tiffany beautifully reframes seasons of suffering not as divine punishment, but as divine invitation into deeper knowledge of the only One who can heal, deliver, and restore. Throughout the entire book, I found myself internally shouting, 'Yes and amen!' with tears rolling down my face, as I experienced the Lord's presence, conviction, and hope. I encourage everyone to journey with Tiffany 'into the wilderness' and into a fresh encounter with Jesus.

Rev. Alicia R. Jackson, PhD.
Associate Professor of Old Testament, Vanguard University

into the wilderness

UNCOVERING HOPE IN YOUR DARKEST SEASONS

TIFFANY NESBITT

Copyright © 2024 by Tiffany Nesbitt
Published by Streamroots
63 Via Pico Plaza #201, San Clemente CA 92672

Author's website: www.streamroots.com

All rights reserved.

No part of this book may be reproduced in any form or by any electronic or mechanical means, including information storage and retrieval systems, without written permission from the author, except for the use of brief quotations in a book review. Unless otherwise noted, scripture quotations are from The ESV® Bible (The Holy Bible, English Standard Version®), © 2001 by Crossway, a publishing ministry of Good News Publishers. Used by permission. All rights reserved.

Cover by Chris Nesbitt

ISBN: 978-0-9993679-5-7 (paperback)
ISBN: 978-0-9993679-6-4 (hardcover)

Printed in the United States of America

study guide

For deeper study, a companion study guide is available for purchase at www.wilderness.quest

Study Guide: www.wilderness.quest

A free sample of the study guide is available here:

Free Sample: www.itw.studyguide.download

acknowledgments

It is an honor to offer my heart's gratitude to those who have journeyed in community with me to this moment. Your love fuels me forward.

To those who were obedient to deliver a prophetic word of encouragement or exhortation: Your words ring in my spirit. Thank you for your risky faith.

To those who gave of their time to read early scribblings: Your honesty has humbled me. Thank you for your sacrifice.

To those who challenged my notions of what was good enough: I am so grateful for the prodding. Thank you for speaking the truth in love.

To those who called out life and identity over my desert places: You have been the transformative hands and feet of Jesus. Thank you for lifting my head and shaping my worldview.

To those who challenged me to step boldly into more: You have made me uncomfortable in the best way. Thank you for being a friend who sticks closer than a brother.

To my beta girls: You have transformed this work, and your investment is Heaven's gift. Thank you for your willingness to serve me so lavishly.

To those who provided a quiet space of retreat: Your generosity allowed this book to take shape. Thank you for freely partnering in my labor.

In the words of Jane Austen, *"Now for the cream"*.

To my family: You are my heart's delight and my living legacy. Thank you for believing in me and urging me forward when necessary. I love you.

To my husband: Although *my* name is on the cover of this book, this is *our* story. You have always been *the one* and forever will be. Thank you for making this happen on every level. I adore you.

To my Savior: Thank you, *Abba*. This book is nothing but a journal of Your passionate pursuit of my heart. All glory to you, Jesus—*Soli Deo Gloria*.

Dedicated to Diane Elaine Nesbitt
1941 - 2024
Mother-in-love, spiritual momma, legacy builder.
Your joy never failed to sweeten my wasteland wanderings.

contents

Introduction	13
1. Allure Me	23
2. The Wilderness of Endurance	41
3. The Wilderness of Grace	61
4. Hundredfold Fruit	83
5. A Door of Hope	101
6. Your Love Song	123
7. Lean on Your Beloved	141
About the Author	161
Also by Tiffany Nesbitt	163

introduction

"Be surprised by joy, be surprised by the little flower that shows its beauty in the midst of a barren desert, and be surprised by the immense healing power that keeps bursting forth like springs of fresh water from the depth of our pain."

Henri J.M. Nouwen

When Jesus drew me into the wilderness, I was religious and somewhat idealistic.

Christianity was the foundation of my upbringing and that of my Jesus-loving parents and their parents before them. As a result, I have cherished an honest-to-goodness love for God since surrendering my heart to Him at age seven. But as I matured, that devotion became mixed with a hearty dose of formulaic religiosity. Blended with my genuine affection for the Lord was a twisted sense of performance, a stream of whispered lies.

You're not enough.

You need to work harder, do more for God. Then you'll be fully accepted by Him, fully loved.

In my quest for this conditional affection, I assumed that my spiritual formula for God's favor would protect me from ever having to experience more than a cursory tour of the wilderness. It was supposed to provide a spiritual "free pass," one which would enable me to ride through life in an air-conditioned off-roader, gaping like a tourist at any encounter with a Sonoran landscape.

"Gasp—is that ... cacti?! And just look at the heat steaming from those massive boulders (crank the A/C and flip perfectly coiffed hair)!"

I pitied the folks who found themselves wandering in an arid season because I was convinced that my formula entitled me never to have to step foot into that spiritual landscape. It safeguarded me from the wilderness, a convoluted religious conviction which ran something like:

> A: *I give my heart to Jesus, chasing after a relationship with Him*

> B: *I honor Him with good works, laying down my life for His Kingdom*
>
> C: *God blesses me, gives me the desires of my heart, and keeps me from serious suffering*

I had plenty of double-underlined scriptures to back up this mixed-up theology, so I had always assumed it to be gospel truth. After all, up until that point, none of my experiences had provided a challenge to that paradigm.

Until the wilderness.

With my first stumble into that wasteland, I knew that something was off.

For a long while, I couldn't pin it down. Because my self-concocted conviction had never failed to sum up my experiences with Jesus, I hadn't questioned its legitimacy. So as I trekked through the desert, sweating and suffering, I turned to my circumstances to provide an explanation for the searing heat that caused me to question the bedrock of my faith.

How can a God who ignores my formula possibly be good?

I've wholeheartedly served Him—why would He allow me to suffer?

Miraculously, as I grappled to find answers to my queries, I came face to face with the passionate love of Jesus.

INTRODUCTION

Unlike my own journey, for many of you, the road through the wilderness isn't defined by wrestling with the wrong theology. Instead, that pathway acts as an aching reminder of pain long past. Maybe you've skirted the same boulders before, and the last time, it wasn't pretty. The only testimony which those standing stones give is to your shame: the places you blew it, the mistakes you made. Or perhaps, they act as monuments to the darkness of depression or the horror of abuse. And the last thing you're willing to do is cross the threshold of a hard-earned stability for a glimpse into what you've worked so desperately to leave behind. Even the longing for Jesus' love may not feel like incentive enough to scale the barriers of your heart, because you're convinced that redemption is nothing more than an antiquated fairy tale.

It's so easy for our eyes to become locked on the difficulty of our circumstances. However, if we momentarily shift our perspective and peer into the heavenlies, we uncover a different narrative: a tale of wooing, of redemption so profound and pervasive that it leaves us astounded by its beauty.

Most of us avoid a wilderness season like the plague, skirting it every which way, employing heroic gymnastics to keep even our toes from touching the sand of suffering. And all the while, we're either desperately declaring that Jesus would never take us down that

INTRODUCTION

road, or we're scared to death that wasteland desolation is exactly where we're headed. And if He's such a good God, how could He possibly ask that of us?

But when Jesus gently draws us, it's never about the heartache of the desert. Although gravel and prickly pear may be our landscape, He hasn't led us there to take twisted pleasure in watching us suffer. The heart of Jesus longs to set us free into deepest intimacy with Himself. He desires to cleanse us of hopelessness, shattering every shackle of fear and shame. When at last we choose to grasp His outstretched palm, allowing Him to lead us into the wilderness, He begins a wooing process which puts every earthly lover to shame.

Because your wilderness season does not define you.

You will come out on the other side. Jesus will lead you out of your wasteland into the abundance of hope fulfilled, and when He does, those waves of searing heat which threatened to melt your hope into a desert mirage will vanish. Instead, you'll be feasting on the sweetness of Promise Land fruit, hand in hand with the Lover of your soul.

And your heart will never be the same.

into the wilderness

"'Therefore, behold, I will allure her, and bring her into the wilderness, and speak tenderly to her. And there I will give her her vineyards and make the Valley of Achor a door of hope. And there she shall answer as in the days of her youth, as at the time when she came out of the land of Egypt. And in that day, declares the Lord, you will call me "My Husband," and no longer will you call me "My Baal." For I will remove the names of the Baals from her mouth, and they shall be remembered by name no more. And I will make for them a covenant on that day with the beasts of the field, the birds of the heavens, and the creeping things of the ground. And I will abolish the bow, the sword, and war from the land, and I will make you lie down in safety. And I will betroth you to me forever. I will betroth you to me in righteousness and in justice, in steadfast love and in mercy. I will betroth you to me in faithfulness. And you shall know the Lord.'"

Hosea 2:14-20

ONE
allure me

> "So we have come to know and to believe the love that God has for us. God is love, and whoever abides in love abides in God, and God abides in him."
>
> 1 John 4:16

WITHIN EVERY WOMAN, there is an intense longing to be wooed.

Most of us dream of this fairy tale pursuit from the time we first wriggle into a glittery dress, puffy with iridescent skirts and accessorized with slip-on heels. With a row of dolls for a captive audience, we recite the dream which has been rehearsed by girls for generations.

I am a beautiful princess! My handsome prince is coming to whisk me into his arms, carrying me away on his fear-

less steed. He will welcome me to his castle, where we'll live together happily ever after.

For centuries, crooners and poets have described our hearts' yearning for *The Pursuit*. From Shakespeare's immortal *Romeo and Juliet* to Taylor Swift's rockin' country ballad, *Love Story*, the longing for lasting love has been recounted throughout history.

For a handful of women, that girlish fantasy becomes a reality. But most of us crash hard into the truth that puffy skirts fall painfully short of real beauty. And the handsome prince? Well, let's just say that he forgot both his steed and the castle deed in the land of fairy tales, because that legendary bliss just doesn't last.

But our longing to be pursued won't be silenced.

No matter how much we've been disappointed or betrayed, disillusioned, or abandoned, there remains in our hearts an almost unrecognizable whisper of *what if?*

What if there was a man who pursued me, who laid down his own life to choose me? What if he stuck around and was faithful to ordinary, unremarkable me? What if I could be loved like that, right through all the mundane and the I-want-to-quit moments?

So often, however, our desire is shushed by an auto playlist of our failures, rotating on repeat in our minds: *I'm way too (fill in the blank) to be loved like that.*

Most of us are convinced it would take some otherworldly combination of Superman, Mr. Darcy, and William Wallace to conquer our impenetrable walls of guilt, shame, and insecurity, loving us passionately and faithfully in the midst of the mess we're convinced we are.

THE PROPHET AND THE PROSTITUTE

Enter Hosea.

One of those little-read minor prophets, Hosea is an Old Testament book of the Bible which describes *The Pursuit* in a way that can be mind-blowing.

Hosea lived in the soon-to-be-conquered nation of Israel around the middle of the 8th century B.C. Hosea 1:2 tells us that *"the Lord ... spoke through Hosea."* In other words, God gave him prophetic downloads for his countrymen, sharing His heart with Hosea in such a way that his fellow Israelites would hopefully hear and understand. Being a prophet of the Most High God at any point during Israel's tumultuous history was a tough gig. Ridicule, persecution, imprisonment—even violent death—were all common hazards of the occupation. So when the word of the Lord came to Hosea, I'm sure he must have taken time to count the cost, especially considering his first assignment.

At the outset of the book, God commands Hosea to marry a prostitute by saying, *"Go, take yourself a wife of whoredom and have children of whoredom, for the land commits great whoredom by forsaking the Lord"* (Hosea 1:2b).

Who—me, Lord?

Hosea's mission must have chafed hard against all he thought he knew of God's instructions for holy living. In ancient times, prostitutes were viewed by polite society as the most contemptible of women, lower than low—certainly not marriage material for a kosher Jewish boy who was also a prophet of God. Hosea's divine assignment undoubtedly stirred a righteous revulsion within his heart.

Repulsed as he may have been, Hosea obeys the Lord's voice. Verse 3 reports, *"So he went and took Gomer, the daughter of Diblaim, and she conceived and bore him a son."* In spite of his wrestlings, Hosea obediently chooses a woman who possesses the necessary qualifications. Gomer is redeemed from the slavery of prostitution and established as his wife by covenant.

At this point in the narrative, it's tempting to let scenarios spin as we consider the unspoken details of this improbable romance. Had Hosea spotted Gomer in the marketplace? Noticed her as she sauntered the streets, hips swaying? Perhaps he had wrestled to avert his eyes, knowing well the warnings of Solomon regarding an immoral woman. The motive of his particular choice isn't mentioned in Scripture; nevertheless, out of all the disreputable women of his region, he chooses Gomer. Hardened by sin and wounded by the degradation of innumerable sexual encounters, she is brought under the protection of Hosea's love.

Eventually, a family is born to the couple: two sons and a daughter, all intentionally named by God to represent Israel's sin and His heart towards His people. But despite any inherent love for her children, Gomer eventually runs. Scripture doesn't reveal the motive of her heart; we're left only with speculation. Perhaps she was never able to grasp her true worth, unable to see herself as anything other than a woman of the streets. Maybe she felt inescapably tied to a man for whom she felt no real tenderness or gratitude. Regardless of her motive, she abandons her family for the irresistible draw of her former life. Rejecting the covering of love that Hosea offers, Gomer returns to selling chunks of her soul as she surrenders her body.

Although I've been reading my Bible since my early teens, I didn't give serious consideration to Hosea's saga until diving into Francine Rivers' masterpiece, *Redeeming Love*. Like 99.99% of those who read her fictional account of Hosea and Gomer, I wept my way through it in two days, bawling like a baby at the climax. After scooping up a box's worth of soggy tissues, I realized my curiosity had been piqued. I dove into the biblical story, noticing for the first time the intentionally selfless sacrifice which the Father asked of Hosea.

After being deserted by the mother of his three children, Hosea receives instructions from the Lord, *"Go again, love a woman who is loved by another man and is an adulteress, even as the Lord loves the children of Israel, though they turn to other gods and love cakes of raisins" (Hosea 3:1)*. Although biblical scholars disagree about the identity of the woman mentioned in this verse, many lean towards the conviction that God is asking Hosea to redeem his adulterous wife.

Go AGAIN, Lord?

I don't think I can handle that pain.

But go, he does.

> *"So I bought her for fifteen shekels of silver and a homer (6 bushels) and a lethech (110 liters) of barley. And I said to her, 'You must dwell as mine for many days. You shall not play the whore, or belong to another man; so will I also be to you.'"*
> Hosea 3:2-3

OUR RESPONSE

It's easy for most of us to relate to Hosea. Asked by the Lord to lay down his religious sensibilities and personal desires in order to walk in obedience, he's betrayed and abandoned, left with a young family to raise. He endures gut-wrenching suffering at the hand of the one he has been called to sacrificially love, a wound with which so many of us can empathize.

But what about Gomer?

While not all of us wrestle with a backstory that brings us shame, every one of us has experienced the humiliation attached to poor choices. And I've yet to find a woman who sincerely believes that she's worthy of selfless, redeeming love just as she is. Most of us squirm uncomfortably with the idea of revealing our true selves under the scrutiny of genuine affection. It can feel terrifyingly risky to open our hearts to intimacy with someone who's been exposed to our many faults.

However, Gomer's story is the key to the narrative of Hosea. Throughout the entirety of the book, the Lord shines an allegorical spotlight on Hosea's unfaithful wife. And although Gomer is only mentioned by name in two of the fourteen chapters of his prophecy, the nation which she represents is repeatedly described.

Israel has been a faithless lover, running after other gods and abandoning the One who chose her as His beloved bride. From beginning to end, Hosea expresses the heart of God, lamenting over the sin and treachery of Israel. Even as He reminds Israel of the consequences attached to her choices, He repeatedly declares His steadfast, unfailing love, attempting to woo her back to Himself.

Similar to Hosea, I've wrestled deeply with self-satisfied religion, which caused me to struggle in having compassion for those whose choices challenged my convictions. I've grappled with the need to forgive those who betray me, often reluctant to set aside my pride. I've also grieved over the needless pain inflicted by the self-destructive actions of others. Like Gomer, I've examined my array of past choices and judged myself unworthy, repeatedly. I've felt the temptation to run from commitment, seriously considering abandoning the concept of self-sacrifice—a crucial element for lasting love. The lens of failure and the filter of inadequacy have colored my perception of myself too many times to count.

However, each time I'm ensnared in hopeless sin, Jesus chases me down with His unfailing goodness.

I WILL ALURE HER

After opening with a brief account of his own story, Hosea moves into a prophetic pronouncement of the Lord's heart for Israel. He recounts their history together, calling to mind the many times in which the nation has turned its back on God. It's a hard exposé of the murky choices that have divided their hearts, luring her to break her marriage covenant.

Similarly to our own stories, as we read about Gomer's and Israel's parallel struggles, it's tempting to become entangled in the despondency caused by the sin that trapped them both. When Hosea announces that Israel has rebelliously pursued other lovers and forgotten the Lord, it's weighty—a type of rebuke that should prompt Israel to turn and repent. But she doesn't.

Just when Israel's narrative is beginning to feel like an assured tragedy, verse 14 turns a corner with a phrase that shifts my perspective.

> *"Therefore, behold, I will allure her..."*

The first time I truly encountered that phrase, it brought me to a halt. I had been studying Hosea as a part of my daily time with Jesus, and although I was already acquainted with the book's storyline, I had never fully grasped the transition outlined in that verse. So, I had to pause and read it again.

I will allure her.

Our postmodern understanding of the word *allure* often sparks images of a lusty temptress or ne'er-do-well rogue intentionally plotting to take advantage of an innocent victim. But the actual definition of the word is surprising. Noah Webster, author of *Webster's Dictionary*, defines *allure* in his original 1828 edition:

> "To attempt to draw to; to tempt by the offer of some good, real or apparent; to invite by something flattering or acceptable; as, rewards *allure* men to brave danger. Sometimes used in a bad sense, to *allure* to evil; but in this sense entice is more common. In Hosea 2:14, *allure* is used in its genuine sense..."

Webster himself states that Hosea 2:14 uses the word in its genuine sense, which means that at the time of his writing almost two hundred years ago, allure meant something in the English language which was best typified by that verse. It was the idea of someone attempting to draw something or someone else to themselves, offering some real or apparent benefit as an inducement. So when we're allured, we are pulled towards something or someone by the offer of genuine good.

Let's break this down.

Most days, dark chocolate seems pretty darn alluring. I'm inevitably drawn to its gravitational pull for months on end, convinced it has so much good to offer. Its smoky-sweet flavor, the way it melts in my mouth, not to mention the endorphins which are released every time I savor it—all these temptations act like a siren call to my taste buds. But the indisputable fact is that dark chocolate, while potentially providing a few minor health benefits, has no actual allure, because the only real good it provides is a single moment of bliss. In the end, the button on my jeans declares the shocking truth: I've been suckered once again, duped. Fooled by its heavenly flavor, I forget in a moment of sheer delight that it has no allure. In reality, I've been enticed, and I pay the price in sweat at the gym.

Webster describes *entice* in this way:

> "To incite or instigate, by exciting hope or desire; usually in a bad sense; as, to *entice* one to evil. Hence, to seduce; to lead astray; to induce to sin, by promises or persuasions. To tempt."

As Webster himself knew, our heavenly Father never entices us. Unlike dark chocolate or anything else which can tempt us towards disappointment, He never pulls a bait-and-switch. Because He's the very personification of goodness, Jesus allures us, drawing us towards Himself with the offer of what He alone possesses.

The apostle Paul declares in Romans 2:4 that the kindness of our God is so great, it actually has the power to turn us from our sin and draw us towards His heart in repentance. So He intentionally allures us, captivating our hearts, because He knows that if we respond to His wooing, we'll be immersed in the goodness of a radical, fully satisfying love such as our hearts have never known.

When the Father asks Hosea to pursue Gomer, purchasing her for himself, He is painting an allegorical masterpiece. And when Gomer deserts her husband, returning to her sin and choosing other lovers, God allows Hosea's personal heartache to sound a cry to Israel of His own breaking heart. Most importantly, when the Father instructs Hosea to choose searing self-sacrifice and redeem an adulterous wife, He demonstrates His unfailing love and goodness—a love that allures us right past shame and sin; a goodness that chases us down and doesn't let go. What undoubtedly seemed to Gomer to be too good to be true is found infallible by millions of hearts who respond to Jesus' alluring love.

Almost three thousand years later, He's still pursuing us.

What the Father demonstrated in sending His Son to die in our place was the pinnacle of *The Pursuit*. It's an indelible moment in history, one which can't be superseded or minimized. When we give our *yes* to His love story, we're brought under His covering and fully redeemed from the hopelessness and death of sin. We're allured by His love, and nothing will ever be the same.

But like Gomer, for most of us, that's just the beginning. Just as she struggled with her rescue and redemption, so we also wrestle with receiving the fullness of Jesus' incomprehensible love.

A YEARNING FOR INTIMACY

About ten years ago, Jesus started to draw me with His love in a way I had never known before. At that point, I had been a Christian for thirty years, and I naively believed that I had already marked the "Love of God" checkbox on my "Things Every Christian Should Know" list when I was a teenager. I understood that Jesus loved me and, for the most part, didn't doubt the truth of that statement. But I had never deeply opened my heart to be allured by His love.

As I was going through my One Year Bible reading in the Song of Solomon, I was captured right from the opening:

> "Let him kiss me with the kisses of his mouth, for your love is better than wine; your anointing oils are fragrant: your name is oil poured out; therefore virgins love you. Draw me after you; let us run. The king has brought me into his chambers."
> Song of Solomon 1:2

As a teenager, I had skipped over the Song of Solomon, warned mistakenly by older believers that "It's not appropriate until you're married." Knowing that it celebrated the joys of married intimacy, I wanted to avoid possible temptation; I passed it by year after year. So, when I dove into the book two decades later, I was startled by what Jesus had waiting for me.

I had learned in high school theology class that in addition to poetically describing a literal marriage between Solomon and his bride, the Song of Solomon is also an allegory of the relationship between Christ and His Church. With that in mind, as I read the Shulamite's description of her lover, I was mindful of a stirring hunger which caught me unaware.

> *Let him kiss me with the kisses of his mouth.*

What did it mean to be so allured by the love of Christ that I yearned for Him to come that close? To feel His breath on my skin, to be caressed by Him? I had no grid for such an intimate, uninhibited longing for Jesus.

For your love is better than wine.

Heady, intoxicating, thrilling. The Shulamite blatantly declares that the love of her betrothed is far better than the rush of the best Bordeaux. All of the sweetness, the exhilaration, and abandon without any of the sting. Had I ever tasted Jesus' love in such a deeply satisfying way?

Your anointing oils are fragrant, your name is oil poured out; therefore, virgins love you.

I remember what it had felt like to wear my husband's jacket in the years when we were dating—each time I slid my arms into its too-long sleeves, I was surrounded by his scent. During that same season, just writing or speaking his name brought me a rush of joy. Did the fragrance of Jesus' presence, the very mention of His name, cause me to become lovesick?

Draw me after you, let us run; the king has brought me into his chambers.

To be alone with Him. To be intimate with His heart, experiencing Him in the deepest way. Did I long to come into His presence, shutting the door behind us, reveling in His undivided attention?

At the beginning of verse 4, Solomon's bride makes an eager request of her lover: *Draw me after you.*

In other words, *allure me.*

Draw me towards yourself in such a way that I can't resist. Don't hold anything back from me—let me see the fullness of who you really are. Then call me to yourself, and I'll chase after you. We'll race together, you and I.

As I took time to meditate on these verses, I was undone. I realized that I had never before experienced Jesus in such intimate communion. True, I had loved Him—loved Him deeply, even. But it was a safe, controlled love, kept tidy and manageable in the box of my religious experience and convictions.

More than that, I became convinced that I had never experienced His love for me in the all-encompassing way which the Shulamite describes. So I began to ask Him, to cry out to Him.

Jesus, take the lid off my boxes. Draw close to me; I long to feel Your presence on my skin. Allure me with Your passionate heart.

As the weeks passed, He responded to my cry. He came

in close— closer than I had ever before known. Closer than I had ever known before. And I began to fall headlong in love with my irresistible Savior. Entranced by His beauty, captivated by His heart.

Hosea 2:14 explains that the Lord intends to allure His wayward bride with His unfailing love. But unlike our pre-packaged fantasy stories, that's not the conclusion of this divine fairy tale. His very next statement brings us face to face with the reality that our Father's love is the embodiment of perfection; not only does He draw us to Himself in thrilling intimacy, but He also purifies us of every contaminant which would keep us from oneness with Him. In His infinite wisdom, the Lord declares that once they are alone, He plans to whisk away His bride for a second honeymoon, choosing as their destination a remote, isolated location: the wilderness.

> *"Therefore, behold, I will allure her, and bring her into the wilderness..."*

Dear one, the time has come to surrender to the pursuit of My love. Those things which have held you back from Me no longer matter in the face of My

abiding passion for you. Let go of your resistance, your defenses. Let go of your natural reasoning which convinces you that this heavenly romance is too good to be true. Let me love you deeply, completely.

I have come to give you life and to give it abundantly. Everything which has whispered the opposite of that truth is a lie. Let Me shatter every deception and make you new.

Step into My arms and find your refuge in the shelter of My wings. I am the safest place, your hiding place. I will never leave you or forsake you. Have I not spoken, and shall it not come to pass? Believe Me for the reality of My love transforming the old into new, for my love changes everything.

TWO

the wilderness of endurance

> *"The desert loves to strip bare."*
> *Saint Jerome*

WHEN MY FAMILY migrated from Texas to the state of Arizona, it was tough on my adolescent heart. To say that I wasn't thrilled about the move would be an understatement.

Although Phoenix had experienced decades of development by the time of our arrival, it was still a shock to this southern girl. Saguaro cacti, Jumping Cholla, and a host of other arid plants looked like alien lifeforms to my Texan eyes. Jagged, russet-colored mountains encircled the valley, dividing subdivisions and redirecting thoroughfares all over town.

But the most blatant characteristic of the valley was its lack of vibrant color. Having been raised in the burbs of Dallas, I had a preference for the smallish hills and wide green fields of the Texas plains. In contrast, the rusty shades of my new surroundings convinced me that my family had taken up residence in a barren no-man's land.

Gradually, my perspective began to alter. The desert unfolded its secrets, and I was changed. Breathtaking sunsets, stunning vistas, and magnificent springtime blooms—a canvas of latent beauty spread before me. I just had to have eyes to see it.

The desert is also where I met and married my husband. But in spite of its sentimental value, Phoenix is one location that never merits a top ten spot on my vacation list. And I've yet to experience a single bride who gushes over an upcoming honeymoon to the Sahara, no matter how adventurous she may be.

However, Hosea explains that God harbors an intentional motive for choosing the wilderness for a tryst with His new bride. I love the phrasing of Hosea 2:14 from *The Message*, "I'm taking her back out into the wilderness where we had our first date, and I'll court her."

Most of us scratch our heads as we read those words. Of all the places to regain His bride's trust and affection, the wilderness seems the least likely choice. But this

God who declares Himself to be an unrivaled lover isn't satisfied with our cultural ideas of intimacy. He alone understands the value of the desert for the heart of the one He loves. So He plans a journey for His bride with one purpose in mind: to court her.

CUTTING COVENANT

Barren and inhospitable, the desert surrounding the backside of Mount Sinai is home today only to roaming tribes of Egyptian Bedouins. But in spite of the harsh environment, streams of pilgrims continue to trek to the spot where God sealed His promise of love with the children of Israel. Almost four thousand years ago, it became the holy ground for God to *karath beriyth*—literally in the Hebrew, to *cut covenant*—with man.

Shrouded in darkness, God declares to Moses from the heights of the mountain: *"You yourselves have seen what I did to the Egyptians, and how I bore you on eagles' wings and brought you to myself. Now therefore, if you will indeed obey my voice and keep my covenant, you shall be my treasured possession among all peoples, for all the earth is mine; and you shall be to me a kingdom of priests and a holy nation..." (Exodus 19:4-6b).*

With these words, the King of the universe takes His treasured bride, instigating a legal and binding covenant.

I WILL.

Israel has just spent three months being courted by a God who has turned their world upside down. He's displayed His strength, delivering the Israelites through the Red Sea. He's proven Himself as a provider, raining bread from heaven. And He's demonstrated His power, causing water to rush from a rock.

So, they pledge themselves fervently.

We will.

As Moses clambers up the mountain to receive the terms of the covenant, known by biblical scholars as the Mosaic law, God's glory descends upon the mountain in a cloud of devouring fire, consummating the holy ceremony.

The vows are spoken, and the marriage is sealed. It's time for the Bridegroom to whisk away His beloved. The Lord honeymoons His bride in the desert, yet even as He woos her, she yearns for lesser lovers.

PURIFYING HEAT

As much as I might protest otherwise, those rebellious wanderers are far too relatable. The Israelites' cravings for chunky Egyptian cuts of meat and their pantheon of idols are longings which may have manifested themselves differently in the ancient world, but in actuality, they're rooted in yearnings which are universal.

Let's face it: the desires of our flesh are enticing.

And the desert causes my flesh to manifest in intriguing ways. The intense heat causes me to sweat in a most unladylike manner. Damp circles underline my pits. Beads of sweat form a mustache on my upper lip. Trickles of perspiration stream down my back, saturating my unmentionables. It's not a pretty sight. However, the sweat serves a significant purpose. It not only regulates my body's temperature, enabling me to endure a harsh climate, but it also accomplishes a secondary goal: detoxification. All those toxins in my system, accumulated through poor dietary choices, environmental stresses, and even unhealthy emotional habits, are released as those tiny fountains of perspiration begin to spout.

Similarly, the Lord sees every place where my mind and spirit harbor microbes of sin. Through each of my desert seasons, the Father has turned up the temperature on the poisonous belief tucked deep in my heart that *God is not really good*. Don't get me wrong—it wasn't a conviction I had on display. Just like those toxins lodged in the crevices of my organs, it was hidden, secretly rooted in the secluded places of my mind, unseen even by me. And as the heat rose, that contaminated gunk dripped out of my soul's pores.

Jesus alone perceives the cords of sin wound round my heart, tugging until the very life seems to be squeezed from my chest. He sees the bondage, the lies, the things hidden in shadows. There's no blindness in His passion for me: every aspect of my heart is revealed under His scrutiny of grace. So this wasteland wooing, it's tailor-made—as unique as my fingerprints. My courtship journey is as individual and somehow as universal as my sin.

But in spite of the invitation to freedom which Jesus offers, my first inclination in those wilderness seasons is to run. Everything in my heart and mind screams survival, and I want to bolt back to the land of slavery where my breath reeks of leeks and onions (*Numbers 11:4*). Never mind that I was bound in miserable servitude to those ungodly taskmasters. Just like the Israelites, the challenges of the wilderness can cause me to lose sight of my unfailing source of living water, which in turn causes me to lose my perspective of truth (*Exodus 17:1-7*). When that happens, my fear of the unknown, of embracing wholehearted trust, takes over.

Because the desert strips.

THE PEAKS OF ENDURANCE

Over the years, I've had the privilege of walking alongside other hearts as they've journeyed through the wilderness. With each person, the questions have arrived thick and fast; pre-packaged, religious answers don't offer much comfort. And it's all too easy for me to relate, because every time Jesus has led me into my personal desert seasons, there's been a whole lot of complaining. Grumbling about feeling abandoned. Questioning His goodness and His faithfulness.

All that complaining, grumbling, and questioning has often been spurred by my self-made effort to scale the mountain ridges that pepper the wilderness floor. In the end, I flopped down hard and blubbered like a baby. When my four kids were young, the shower was my favorite griping spot. I'd lock the bathroom door, blast the hot water, and settle under the stream, weeping in the only place I could truly get alone.

Lord, how on earth do You expect me to reach the summit of this peak? I'm physically exhausted and emotionally drained. Have You abandoned me? You were the One who instructed me to climb these hills, Jesus. I never would have taken this journey if it wasn't for You. All You have to do is say the word, and I'll be miraculously rescued. But, no—You insist that I keep climbing! Why have You chosen to lead me this way? Don't You know I'm not conditioned for a journey like this? That chasm You just asked me to leap—I could have plummeted to my death!

I could feel the stripping of my dearest *soul props*—all my ungodly beliefs and habits, which I used to brace up my soul—each time I stepped under the steaming downpour.

Oh, but *endurance*.

It's one of those tidy, biblical words—something everyone seems to want, but no one seems to want to experience. To grow in endurance necessitates ... well, *enduring*.

Can't I give it a miss?

But in His tenderness, right in the moment when hopelessness threatens to strangle me, Jesus makes a holy exchange: my weakness for His strength. My perfectionism for His power. My lack of stick-to-it-iveness for His *endurance*. I trade all of my *soul props*—performance, perfectionism, control, and so many more—for a freedom from striving, from all of the grasping which leads me to the end of my own rope. Every time I'm found dangling on those frayed edges, the Lord throws me a lifeline which looks a lot like Romans 5:3-5:

> "*More than that, we rejoice in our sufferings, knowing that suffering produces endurance, and endurance produces character and character produces hope, and hope does not put us to shame because God's love has been poured into our hearts through the Holy Spirit who has been given to us.*"

Jesus comes courting with whispers of hope:

Embrace endurance. It's my gift to you, beloved. The pathway to hope.

This is the crux of the matter, the heart of what the Father longs to impart to my spirit. The suffering, the feeling of overwhelming weakness, it's so multi-faceted and, in a word ... glorious. To fully understand my helplessness is to grasp the depth of God's power at work in me.

Strong's Concordance provides a broader understanding of the apostle Paul's description of weakness:

> *astheneia* (Greek): *Want of strength, weakness, infirmity of the body; feebleness of health or sickness of soul; to bear trials and troubles.*
>
> *"For when I am weak, then I am strong."*
> 2 Corinthians 12:10b

To be *astheneia* is to be strong. And this strength is so much more than just the raw emotional energy to crawl through the day. When I embrace the truth that God's strength is discovered in my deepest areas of weakness, I step into the gift which the Holy Spirit has been offering since salvation—the *dunamis* power of God.

> *dunamis* (Greek): *Inherent power, residing in a*

thing by virtue of its nature; power for performing miracles; moral power and excellence of soul; power and influence which belong to riches and wealth; power and resources arising from numbers; power resting upon armies or hosts.

Each time I embrace my weakness, I'm actually embracing the opportunity to realize all this power perfected in me: His miracles, His sanctification, His excellence, His riches, His influence, His resources, His victorious power.

When I encounter Him on those rugged mountainsides, I'm captivated by His strength, enamored by this offering of hope. The way He rescues me from perfectionism and the demands of striving can't help but make my heart thrill. As I grow in endurance, it becomes the wellspring of strength that I so desperately need to ascend those sheer walls. It's that endurance-which-births-hope which propels me to the other side of the wilderness as *"more than a conqueror" (Romans 8:37).*

THE WILDERNESS OF LACK

But the wilderness isn't just riddled with razor-edged obstacles; it's also characterized by its scarcity.

Have you ever watched one of those National Geographic documentaries, videos which highlight insects or toads that are able to endure the harsh conditions of their habitat through crazy, God-given strategies? There's a key reason for those instinctual survival tactics. The sandy floor of the desert yields little to sustain life. The lack of food, water, and shelter calls for creative and sometimes desperate measures to ensure existence.

Each time the Holy Spirit woos me into the wilderness, the blatant lack which characterizes that territory can threaten to overwhelm my perspective. As I scratch at the sand, desperate to uncover a morsel of sustenance, my heart is left vulnerable to fear, distrust, and hopelessness.

For the Israelites, God's daily provision of manna miraculously sustained them throughout their forty-year trek. And yet they grumbled about the very nutrition which kept them alive (*Exodus 16; Numbers 11:1-19*). Their daily ration was carefully prescribed according to the size of their household, and anyone who tried to gather more than their allotted portion soon uncovered rottenness in his tent. But it wasn't stinginess which caused God to stipulate specific allotments. It was a test of their hearts: the chance to choose contentment in the daily sustenance.

I'm convinced that Jesus has a real sense of humor, because my modern-day manna has often tasted surprisingly like ... peanut butter. During one of our hardest wilderness seasons, my grumblings crept their way into my journal.

I flip open the cupboard for the sixth time today, peering into the recess. And for the sixth time, the same jar of peanut butter meets my eye: Kirkland creamy, unopened.

That's it.

I want to sit and howl. Or better yet, lay on my belly, kicking like an indignant toddler.

This is not how things were supposed to go. The correct game plan has already been crafted—by me. *I trust God for His leading and direction. I step out in obedience, believing in His miraculous provision. Jesus shows up and provides abundantly, displaying His power and getting the glory.*

Remember, God? We had a deal.

I've marched around this mountain before. The landscape looks uncomfortably familiar. Same shrubs and scrub. Same dry-as-dust hills. *And last time we were here, Lord, remember how this ended? Not too pretty. These eleventh-hour rescues of Yours ... not a fan.*

It's not that I don't enjoy peanut butter. But come on —all things in moderation, right? And peanut butter does leave something to be desired. All that sticky mess on the roof of your mouth with no milk to wash it down ... *ugh*.

I much prefer leeks and onions.

And You promised provision, remember?

This manna business is getting old. I close the cupboard and move towards greener pastures.

Mounds of laundry greet me, each heaped up like the pile I carry on my back, the weight of the wrestling. I'm weary, and I'm done.

A little quail in the mix might be nice, Lord. You know, something to break the monotony ... 'cause I know You spoke it, but I sure can't spot any milk and honey flowing in this barren space. How long can I stomach this daily bread?

And you promised provision, remember?

In this moment of the common place, I crave the revelation. I need the grace to understand the unspoken answers because the silence is roaring in my ears.

I pair up the socks, black with black and white with white. Piles of black and white are staring at me, and

I'm wishing life's challenges could be compartmentalized so easily. Folded and neatly put away, each in its own tidy space. Formulaic. Simple.

I poke my finger through an unexpected hole. *It's high time for the charis moment,* I think. *The moment of grace. It's been time for a long time.*

Behind my veiled accusation, the revelation hits.

Who holds sovereignty here?

Is it me, with my mile-long list of wants, handily camouflaged as needs? Is it me, with my vision of how it all should run? Is it me, yearning for leeks and onions when what He's given is peanut butter?

What He's given, He always gives. It's Him, the sovereign One.

What Jesus gives rarely matches my checklist. It rarely fits my grand personalized bill of expectation. But He does give. And in His sovereignty, He gives beautifully. He gives more than enough: my breath, my life, my joy, my peace ... one gift poured out upon another. A continuous stream of unending generosity, liquid love.

But in my longing to wrest the crown and play the part, I demand from Him what I think I need, what He should know I need. And He whispers back.

What I have given is always enough. There is always more than enough of Me, the Bread of Life.

Can I look at that lone jar of peanut butter and embrace it as the more-than-enough provision of my all-knowing Lord? Can I say *yes* to the fresh supply of what I need, rather than whine for what I want?

I drop the socks and muse the question.

In the space of quiet, I build an altar. Like the patriarchs of old, I'm taking the ground of this dusty, day-to-day earth and consecrating it as sanctified in the presence of the Holy One. I wrestle the offering onto the altar; pride doesn't die easily.

You are sovereign, Abba. I choose You, my Daily Bread.

The socks are folded in close packets, all jumbled on top of one another in a glorious heap of finished disarray. It's supper time.

Hello, peanut butter.[1]

This battle to trust has so often floored me. Countless times my closet has become the ring for my wrestling matches with Jesus. Each time I've been toe to toe with Him, teeth fiercely clenched, He's gone down to the mat with me, embracing me tightly. Because His covenant with me is eternal, Jesus is never willing to let me go. Only when I finally cry "*Uncle!*" does He gently peel the fear of lack, of not enough, of what-if-He-doesn't-come-through out of my clenched hands.

And when I yield, the bonds of fear miraculously disintegrate. The rain of the Spirit washes my heart clean from every stronghold of lack, that orphan mindset which tries to convince me that my Father isn't truly trustworthy—that He will abandon me or won't come through in my time of need. When I'm set free from those lies, I glance down and notice fragrant blossoms of joy springing from the dirt, overtaking the prickly pear and pebbles which littered the ground only moments prior.

THE WASTELAND OF ISOLATION

For many, the desert's greatest hardship is not found in its obstacles or lack, but in its isolation.

A honeymoon is designed only for two. And when one half of the couple is the invisible God—seen only through eyes of faith, heard in the merest whisper of a still, small voice—it can be a fight to protect our hearts from the lie of abandonment. Because for some of us, the thing which causes us to tremble most violently is the idea of being left alone, lost in the caverns and canyons of an inhospitable barrenness.

Something about Jesus' wooing can feel so backward and upside down to our earthly sensibilities. He intentionally leads us into the places we fear the most, expressly for the purpose of demonstrating the most powerful revelations of His heart.

My most miserable experience with desert isolation is ingrained in my memory. My husband and I were smack-dab in the middle of a crushing five years; we weren't catching sight of a reprieve any time soon. With our oldest son away at school, we had lived as a family of five in eighteen homes within eleven months—for the first time in our lives, we were wholly dependent on the good grace of those who loved us. We were financially spent—many days, putting five dollars in the gas tank was a major stretch—and we were wondering what on earth Jesus was doing with our crazy lives. Well-meaning onlookers were offering all the opinions about our heart motives and choices, some labeling us as unrooted, idealistic, presumptuous idlers. The pain was deep.

With this as my backdrop, I was returning home one evening from a trip to Costco after valiantly attempting to stretch my pennies beyond their capacity. I was emotionally wiped out. As I exited the freeway in my falling-apart car, I glanced to my left. Seated in the shiny new Range Rover next to me, a family of four chatted animatedly about events of the day, oblivious to my pain. In that moment, the enemy's lie knocked the spiritual wind right out of me, sounding deceptively like the woebegone train of my own thoughts.

I don't think anyone has a clue what it's like to be in my shoes. In fact, no one I know has gone through this particular package of suffering, so no one can truly walk this journey with me. I'm completely alone.

Right in the middle of my titanic pity party, Jesus had oh-so-lovingly positioned me for a powerhouse breakthrough. As I wept in the car, feeling isolated and abandoned by the One who had already cut covenant with me, I was finally ready to see.

> "I will **never** leave you or forsake you."
>
> "I will never **leave** you or forsake you."
>
> "I will never leave you or **forsake** you."
>
> Deuteronomy 31:6

Trembling behind the steering wheel, I had to ask myself: *do I really believe His promise?*

When I feel so lonely that my heart splits open to its core, what do I truly trust: the bullying voice of my circumstances, or the steadfast whisper of His covenantal love?

It's in those moments when I've collapsed onto the dust

of the desert floor, all alone with my questions and doubts—completely alone with Him—that I've finally grasped the truth: His heart beats only for me.

THE JOY OF THE PURSUIT

What does *The Pursuit* look like? It's all of the rapture and delight of tasting the love of our magnificent God. It's the joy of being gifted with everything we don't deserve by the One who knows us better than we know ourselves. But so much more, the wooing of Jesus means uncovering a well of supernatural endurance, strength, and provision. It's the understanding that His presence alone provides the companionship which I need to thrive. And with those gifts of realization comes freedom. Freedom to embrace everything which is truth: my identity, my inheritance, and my destiny.

When Jesus speaks His words of love, everything shifts. And His pursuit carries with it the tenderest of whispers meant for my ears alone.

Dear one, the wilderness will not be your grave, so cast off your shroud of grief. I am setting you free to dance and sing. I will take you to the heights, and you will look upon the good land which I have given you. You will come into your inheritance, this is your birthright as My daughter.

Do not allow fear to bind your heart to inaction. Do not be afraid, but step forward and continue to move further with Me. I treasure your faith.

I have engraved your name upon the palm of My hand. You are never out of My sight. I am the One who will do it. I will accomplish it on your behalf.

Move in rhythm with the beat of My heart. Your ears will hear a word behind you saying, "This is the way you should go. Walk in it."

Promised-land power and authority are yours. Come into the fullness of all that I have for you. This is the time; this is the season.

---

1. Tiffany Nesbitt, 2015, August 20. Leeks, Onions and Peanut Butter. Streamroots. https://streamroots.com/posts/leeks-onions-and-peanut-butter/

THREE

the wilderness of grace

> *"Therefore, behold, I will allure her, and bring her into the wilderness, and speak tenderly to her."*
> Hosea 2:14

> *"A word fitly spoken is like apples of gold in a setting of silver."*
> Proverbs 25:11

THE YEAR my husband and I moved our family from Southern California to Nashville, Tennessee, was like nothing we had ever experienced. After living for twenty years within the same community, the Lord spoke unexpectedly to our hearts, calling us to *"Get up... and go to a land which I will show you" (Genesis 12:1)*. It was a tough word. All four of our children had been born in our tight-knit coastal town. We had spent years investing in our church community, serving and leading. Friends felt like family. And yet, we knew we had to obey the voice of Jesus. So, we sought wisdom from trusted leaders, and once we were convinced that the Lord had indeed spoken, we started packing.

In a single moment, everything shifted. On the highway between Phoenix and Flagstaff, Arizona, a tire exploded on the overloaded car in which my oldest son and I were riding, catapulting our vehicle into the air as we flipped multiple times. While my son miraculously walked away relatively unscathed, I had to be pulled out of the crushed car by the "jaws of life" and transported by Helivac to a hospital in Phoenix. After two surgeries on my right hand and removing glass from my entire body, I was finally able to join my family in our new home in Tennessee.

During the months after our move, things progressed from bad to worse. My husband's business virtually collapsed, leaving us with a minuscule amount of monthly income. As a result, we eventually lost the two houses which we owned. For the first year or two, we had a scanty community as we struggled to find a church which felt like home. I felt confused, scared, and lonely. Morning after morning, I would lay in my bedroom closet, face muffled in the carpet, pouring out my heart to the Lord. Most days, there seemed to be little reply.

For the first year, my husband and I routinely cycled through the same litany of questions: *What have we done wrong? Did we miss the Lord? Are we walking in disobedience? Is there hidden sin in our lives? Are we being punished for something?* Desperate to find answers that the Lord didn't seem to be sharing, we regularly fasted and prayed, both individually and together. We reached out to those who knew us well, hoping to glean nuggets of wisdom to help us navigate our crisis.

Finally, a family member recommended that we meet with a respected Christian leader in the city for counsel. My husband made an appointment, connecting with him over the phone to share our story. At the end of their time together, this well-meaning gentleman offered his conclusion: we had missed God. Somewhere along the way, we must have missed His leading because where God guides, He provides. We needed to repent and seek the Lord, asking Him to reveal where we had taken a wrong turn, and He would graciously forgive, redirect, and bless.

From his perspective, it was simple spiritual math:

$A + B = C$.

We were devastated.

For months we wrestled with this assessment of our lives, trying hard to reconcile our daily heart posture with what had been spoken over us. Crying out to the Lord for wisdom.

NEW WINESKINS

A few months later, I was awakened in the middle of the night by the whisper of the Spirit. As He gently spoke, everything crystallized:

I brought you into the wilderness to transform you into a new wineskin.

I was electrified. As I wept into my pillow, so much of the confusion, pain, and shame started to peel from my heart, like aging paint being stripped from splintered wood. I began talking to Jesus about where He was taking us and why. And my soul, raw and exposed, embraced a twinge of hope.

After sharing the revelation with my husband, we spent weeks studying wineskins—their characteristics and their use in the ancient world. We began meditating on the words of Jesus from Mark 2:18-22, specifically verse 22:

> "And no one puts new wine into old wineskins. If he does, the wine will burst the skins—and the wine is destroyed, and so are the skins. But new wine is for fresh wineskins."

Because the teaching from Mark 2:22 was unique for our

lives in that season, I won't use this space to elaborate on new wineskin properties. However, Jesus' words from the book of Mark do provide a key which is universal.

He loves us that much.

In His infinite wisdom, the Father knew that prior to our journey through the wilderness, our hearts would not have been able to hold the new wine of His Spirit which He longed to pour into us. Like crusty, rigid wineskins, we would have burst from the fresh fermentation, wasting the precious liquid which was meant to saturate our lives with the presence and power of God.

So, He allured us into the wilderness. Hungry for more of Him, willing to chase after Him no matter the cost, we followed the Lord into the heat of the desert. And despite months of seeming silence, He had been storing up words of love which would eventually transform everything for our hearts. At just the right moment, that whispered phrase of truth catapulted us from despair to hope.

Beloved sister, I want to speak life over you.

If your heart beats hard for Jesus, your wilderness is not a punishment.

Let me say that again.

*Your wilderness is **not** a punishment.*

Don't mishear me: if willful or hidden sin is your stumbling block, He *will* allow you to wander through the desert in order to recapture your heart. He'll give you over to the idols you crave until that stuff tastes sickening and loathsome (*Numbers 11:18-20*). But He doesn't do it to punish you.

His single aim is to woo you.

HIS GREAT LOVINGKINDNESS

Romans 1 gives us a blow-by-blow description of the process of hardening our hearts towards God. Through a Spirit-inspired download of wisdom, Paul explains how men and women choose to set themselves up as their own deities, resisting the repeated proofs of Christ's love. Rejecting His authority, they embrace the depravity of sin until their consciences can no longer discern between good and evil.

Chapter 2 takes us directly into an understanding that those who have willfully chosen this path *will* incur the judgment of God. However, Paul then reminds us that it is the great kindness of God which leads us to repentance. It's a kindness upon which we should not presume, but rather by which we should allow our hearts to be broken, softened, and transformed.

> *"Come now, let us reason together, says the Lord: though your sins are like scarlet, they shall be as white as snow; though they are red like crimson, they shall become like wool."*
> Isaiah 1:18

Some biblical scholars link the Greek word which Paul uses for kindness, *chréstotés*, with the Hebrew word *chesed*. *Chesed* is so ripe with meaning that theologians have a difficult time narrowing it down to even a few key definitions. But most Old Testament translations choose the words *steadfast love* or *lovingkindness* to convey its weight. *Chesed* also carries the connotation of *favor, lovely appearance,* and, my personal favorite, *covenantal loyalty.*

The idea of God's covenantal loyalty is one which is repeated throughout the Old Testament; however, for those of us living in the twenty-first century, it can be a difficult concept to grasp. Because it's a notion which seems removed from my daily life, I can stumble over this aspect of God's nature. Webster explains that a covenant is *a coming together of two parties into a like-minded, solemn promise.* But the biblical meaning of cutting covenant is far more than just giving my word. It's a gift of my whole self. It's a commitment to uphold my pledge in spite of the behavior of the other party, fulfilling my promise no matter the cost.

This is how God describes His love for us, His daughters. His loyalty to us is crafted through His covenant of love with us. It's completely dependable—unshakeable. And it's this transparent lovingkindness which draws us to the Father. His very nature is like the pull of the tide, continually beckoning us deeper into His heart.

So, when He speaks to us tenderly, He speaks out of the overflow of His *chesed* for us.

> *"You are altogether beautiful, my love; there is no flaw in you…you have captivated my heart, my sister, my bride; you have captivated my heart with one glance of your eyes, with one jewel of your necklace. How beautiful is your love, my sister, my bride!"*
> Song of Songs 4:7, 9-10a

Jesus' tender whispers of love provide an invitation. We can lean hard into His *chesed*, confident that what might feel like punishment is actually holy preparation. And just like a bride who chooses to confidently trust the leading of her husband, we can find shelter under His covering and rest, secure in the knowledge that He has the details of our desert sojourn already worked out.

> *"My beloved speaks and says to me: 'Arise, my love, my beautiful one, and come away, for behold, the winter is past; the rain is over and gone. The flowers*

appear on the earth, the time of singing has come, and the voice of the turtledove is heard in our land. The fig tree ripens its figs, and the vines are in blossom; they give forth fragrance. Arise, my love, my beautiful one, and come away. O my dove, in the clefts of the rock, in the crannies of the cliff, let me see your face, let me hear your voice, for your voice is sweet, and your face is lovely.'"
Song of Songs 2:10-14

The tranquility of the desert hones our hearing. His words of wooing which might have fallen on deaf ears in our places of prosperity are now our daily bread. And we feed on His steadfast love, His bountiful *chesed*.

"'For the mountains may depart and the hills be removed, but my steadfast love (chesed) *shall not depart from you, and my covenant of peace shall not be removed,' says the Lord, who has compassion on you."*
Isaiah 54:10

LISTENING AND LOVING

In light of His tenderness, how do we rightly handle the pain which can overtake us in our wastelands?

Have you ever experienced the misery of a severe sprain or broken bone? When you're wounded, any thoughtless touch can cause the pain to burn like fire. A competent caregiver will administer medical aid while remaining mindful of a patient's suffering. With the right remedy in place, healing begins; eventually, the shooting pain disappears.

Proverbs 16:24 tells us that *"Gracious words are a honeycomb, sweet to the soul and healing to the bones."*

No matter what words others may have spoken over you, Jesus speaks grace. Because our Father is *Jehovah Rapha*, the God Who Heals *(Exodus 15:26)*, He knows best how to handle your throbbing, wounded heart with the tenderest of care.

Although the role of Jesus' tender words can never be understated, we can't move on without also examining the balm which the words of an earthly comforter are meant to provide. Nowhere in Scripture is this more powerfully illustrated than in the example of Job's three friends.

When Jesus leads the patriarch Job into a wilderness season, He allows Satan to strip him of everything: possessions, children, reputation, and eventually, his physical health. Job is understandably devastated. Yet in the midst of his extreme suffering, and in spite of his wife's foolish counsel to curse God and die, he chooses to give God praise, a posture which positions him for eventual breakthrough *and* complete two-fold restoration.

Upon hearing Job's tragic news, his closest friends hustle over to help. Scripture states that when they catch a glimpse of their old comrade, they don't even recognize him. They weep and wail, tearing their robes in grieving solidarity, and then sit silently in the dust with him for seven days *(Job 1-2)*.

If things had ended there, all might have been well. But at the end of that week, Job opens his mouth to confide in his companions the searing pain of his heart, mind, and body, and everything goes downhill. For twenty-seven chapters, the narrative tosses back and forth between Job verbally writhing in his loss and his three counselors working overtime to fix it all.

To fix *him*.

I have to assume that if Job's friends had been privy to the throne room conversation which super-launched his wilderness season, things would have gone down differently. The Lord's description of Job to Satan is so powerful, I can't pass up the chance to quote it.

> *"And the Lord said to Satan, 'Have you considered my servant Job, that there is none like him on the earth, a blameless and upright man, who fears God and turns away from evil?'"*
> Job 1:8

There is none like him on the earth.

A blameless and upright man.

He fears God and turns away from evil.

I can't even imagine the Lord using that kind of language to describe me. And God isn't being facetious in His description. As a proud Abba, He's taking the opportunity to boast about His son to the evil one, who would love nothing more than to wipe Job off the face of the earth. In His omniscience, the Lord initiates a holy set-up, one which positions Job to display the glory of God through his suffering, a foreshadowing of the death of the spotless Lamb of God.

But in their self-imposed efforts to console and advise their friend, Job's companions not-so-subtly accuse, berate, and belittle him. And as we sit in our cushy armchairs thousands of years later, we often cluck our tongues at those short-sighted men who can't seem to see past the ends of their noses. But the truth is, we can be just like them.

Over the course of her lifespan, the Church has earned herself a reputation for being a Body which shoots her own wounded. That phrase means different things in different situations, but nowhere is it more aptly demonstrated than in the tale of this saint who suffered so much. Job is fully human, full of frailties. But instead of his friends humbly acknowledging their own need for mercy and ministering to his weakness from a place of compassion, they judge in self-righteousness. They speak when they should be silent. And they are silent when they should say the one thing which is most needful: *my heart grieves with you in your suffering. How can I bear your burden?*

Too often, we are just like those comfortless comforters. We speak when we should *just listen*. We offer advice when we should *just pray*. We frequently judge others in a spirit of criticism, all the while commending ourselves for our own godly, prosperous lives—just like the Pharisee of Jesus' day who exclaimed, *"God, I thank you that I am not like other men, extortioners, unjust adulterers, or even like this tax collector. I fast twice a week; I give tithes of all that I get" (Luke 18:11-12).*

To be a friend to someone trekking through the wilderness looks like groaning alongside them in their pain, allowing my cheeks to be smeared with the same tears that streak theirs. It means embracing an understanding that while suffering is universal, each person's journey is also unique in countless ways. Because of that, I should speak words of life without being sanctimonious. I should share the wisdom of the mystery of God, reveling in the truth that while He is always good, He is also always wild. He never fits into my boxes. He doesn't follow my formulas, and His ways are past finding out *(Romans 11:33).*

As the Body of Christ, we must model ourselves after Christ, our Comforter. When Jesus draws us into the desert, His tender words are sweeter than honey, healing every throbbing place of our souls.

Webster's 1828 Dictionary defines *tenderly* as *"mildly; gently; softly; in a manner not to injure or give pain."*

The Darby Translation of Hosea 2:14b records the words *"I will speak tenderly to her"* as *"I will speak to her heart."* This means that the tenderness of God has a second purpose—to draw us near to hear.

HEARING HIS VOICE

Your heart was designed to hear the voice of God. You were created for communion, crafted for intimacy. It's always been the intention of the Father to walk and talk with you, inviting you into the joy of uninhibited fellowship. Over the course of history, multitudes of redeemed men and women have swallowed the lie that hearing from God is a blessing which only uber-spiritual people can access. But the truth is, once you've yielded your life to the lordship of Jesus Christ, you are fully His. And Jesus Himself declares that *His sheep hear His voice*, and they follow Him (*John 10:3-4*).

But the Holy Spirit speaks in a whisper. We often expect that to experience His voice is to find it in the mighty demonstrations of God's power. Like the prophet Elijah, we have to grow in our understanding that the sound of Jesus' call is a gentle sigh, a tender murmur which comes wrapped in His *shalom*, the deep *peace* of God *(1 Kings 19:9-13)*. Cultivating a hearing ear requires patience and time. It necessitates daily moments of waiting on God, allowing His Spirit to cut through the chaos in our lives until all that is left is the gentle nudge of His presence upon our hearts.

The more you quiet your soul, the more clearly you'll hear Him. As you ask the Lord to sweep your thoughts clean, His voice will have the space to enter. This is a daily practice of waiting only on His pleasure, allowing Him to draw you to Himself as you soak in His love. When you entrust the cares of your life into His keeping, the pull of your flesh is quieted, and you become still; suddenly, His tender voice becomes clear.

When I first began listening for the voice of Jesus, I had been a Christian for over twenty years. At that point in my life, I had developed a habit of studying the Word and praying every day, but I often walked away feeling like I was missing something deeper. Because of my spiritual hunger, I was willing to do whatever it took to hear from the Lord. After receiving wise counsel, I bought myself a "listening" journal and just started. I read my Bible, prayed, and then waited in my chair, quietly listening. For days, I had the same sensation that I had experienced at the end of each of my pregnancies, my body thrown into a tizzy with false contractions.

Was that it? Was that you, Lord? Argh ... false alarm—that was definitely not you, Jesus.

Finally, something shifted. I decided to write down all of the impressions which came to my mind and heart during each waiting time. Words, pictures, scriptures, ideas. Anything that *might* be God. Then the next day, I would test it against Scripture, reviewing and praying over it. Before I was even aware, I was learning to discern the voice of the Holy Spirit. I began to recognize the nuances of His voice, the intonations of His words, and the many varied ways in which they lined up with *the* Word. I was discerning what my own inner voice—and even the deceitful voice of the enemy—sounded like in contrast to the gentle, peace-filled whispers of the Spirit. As I stepped out in faith, choosing to believe that I *was* hearing from God, He sweetly confirmed and established my sense of spiritual hearing. And my intimacy with His heart began to explode.

When Jesus speaks to your heart, He does so with one goal in mind: true friendship. He desires nothing more than to be one in fellowship with you *(John 17:20-26)*. Massaging the oil of His Spirit into the crevices of your soul, He oh-so-gently ministers to your aching places, covering them in the healing flood of His precious blood.

But legitimate intimacy is built on trust. And when I'm aching because of the way this journey is playing out—the dusty, shimmering heat, the lack of abundance everywhere, and the just plain *hard*—it's wise to embrace an honest evaluation of my own heart.

DISAPPOINTMENT WITH GOD

A short time after we emerged from that Tennessee wilderness season, I chatted with a woman at the celebration of my goddaughter's wedding. Surrounded by the joy of two lives becoming one, my husband and I had the opportunity to catch up with this acquaintance whom we hadn't seen in years. And she asked, bold-faced, because she understood and she knew.

What have you done about the pain of being disappointed with God?

At that moment, I was thrown back to it all: the pain, the messiness, the season when nothing had seemed right, and everything was upside down. *How could this really be my life?* It was the time when I had felt utterly lost, and no one seemed capable of fixing it. I had felt trapped in a labyrinth with no exit, and the thread to guide me had become so trampled that I could barely distinguish it from the dirt beneath my feet.

As I paused amidst the celebration, struggling to formulate an answer to her question, I was reminded of that same type of pain that had been shared with me by others who had found themselves in wilderness seasons. And of the conviction I had shared with each one.

There are no formulas with God.

He is sovereign, untamed, and perfect in all His ways. Because He is always good, I must choose to lay down my offense upon the altar of surrender and simply trust His goodness.

I recalled again the question of John the Baptizer to his cousin, Jesus. John was languishing in Herod's prison; death was imminent. And he had to know.

Are you the One?

Because I can't see straight for the pain of knowing this is how it might all end. Knowing that hope has been deferred and there may be no way to gather it back. When you descended into the river and the Spirit rested like a dove, I was so certain. But now, hope rots in this cell along with my satchel of unanswered dreams.

Jesus had responded to both John's spoken and unspoken questions.

"Go and tell John what you have seen and heard: the blind receive their sight, the lame walk, lepers are cleansed, and the deaf hear, the dead are raised up, the poor have good news preached to them. And blessed is the one who is not offended by me."
Luke 7:22-23

Jesus was reminding his forerunning cousin of the truth, saying:

I am at work, John. The plans of the Father will be accomplished. Not only am I the Redeemer, but I AM that I AM. Trust me, even when hope seems shattered, for I am the Good Shepherd who lays down his life for his sheep.

I took my time at that wedding and responded to my friend's question. Honestly and simply, I stated the plain fact that the process of surrender can be incredibly difficult. Trusting, even more so. And though the heart is healed, it can still be tender to the touch in those places where the holy scalpel of sanctification has delved deep.

THE WILDERNESS OF GRACE

When we examine the narrative of Hosea, we recognize that we'll never know the full details of Gomer's backstory. However, the threads of ancient history can be woven together to create a tattered tapestry of a street-hardened prostitute, abandoned and abused. Even as Gomer is living in the shame of her perceived worthlessness, she's unexpectedly plucked from the streets by Hosea's act of obedience. But her past pain won't release its grip on her. With its insidious voice sniveling in her ears, she allows the gentler whisper of truth to be swallowed.

And she runs.

Most of us can attest to the fact that pain causes us to react in fear. It causes us to push back, even rejecting the most tender of overtures. It causes us to view our desert through a lens of distrust and abandonment, rather than allowing us to see it for what it truly is: the hidden pathway to intimacy and abundance.

> *"Thus says the Lord: 'The people who survived the sword found grace in the wilderness; when Israel sought for rest, the Lord appeared to him from far away. I have loved you with an everlasting love; therefore, I have continued my faithfulness to you. Again I will build you, and you shall be built, O virgin Israel! Again you shall adorn yourself with tambourines and shall go forth in the dance of the merrymakers. Again you shall plant vineyards on the mountains of Samaria; the planters shall plant and shall enjoy the fruit. For there shall be a day*

when watchmen will call in the hill country of Ephraim: "Arise, and let us go up to Zion, to the Lord our God."""
Jeremiah 31:2-6

In spite of everything that the enemy hollers to the contrary, the Father has crafted the wastelands of your life to be places of great grace. In the midst of hardship, He whispers grace for endurance. In the middle of discouragement and hopelessness, He offers grace for transformation. When loneliness threatens to overwhelm you, He promises the grace for intimacy. And right in the middle of your greatest scarcity, He lavishes you with grace for abundance.

"And there I will give her her vineyards and make the Valley of Achor a door of hope."
Hosea 2:15a

Dear one, you are altogether beautiful. Each time I look at you, My heart starts to beat from just one glance of your eyes. You are radiant in your King's chamber, radiant in My love.

My beloved, it is My love for you that compelled Me to lay down My life. My sacrifice is your sanctification, the genesis of our intimacy. But My love doesn't stop there. Through the supernatural power of resurrection, I took up My life again so that you and I could always be together, never separated. Every time you choose Me, you choose life. Every time you choose My heart over your own ways, you choose joy. I have so much more to give you—mansions and the multitudes of the heavenly host, all resounding with praise to My name.

Come in close. My whisper carries a thousand words of love. Come in closer. I will fight your battles. I will slay your giants. Partner with Me, and watch my breath cause your enemies to flee in countless ways.

Believe Me when I declare that My commitment to you is eternal. Nothing in all of creation can separate you from My love.

FOUR

hundredfold fruit

> *"Let me sing for my beloved my love song concerning his vineyard..."*
>
> Isaiah 5:1

I DON'T REALLY CARE for wine.

It's one of those adult-ish things that I've never learned to enjoy. I was raised in a family where it wasn't served; both of my parents had grown up in church cultures that declared alcohol of any type off-limits. When my husband and I started dating, we realized it was an experience that neither of us relished, so we chose not to start the habit. We were broke; alcohol wasn't cheap. And we were just as content without it.

Since those early years of marriage, I've had dear friends approach me with convincing lines, attempting to persuade me into enjoying the experience that they so obviously relish.

I know you don't enjoy alcohol, but this is different. This is a really nice wine. It's more sweet/more mellow/more flavorful/more expensive/more "whatever" than all the others you may have tried.

Determined that if I can just push past the bitter and the burn, I give it a whirl, posing like a real grown-up who has finally achieved a bit of subtle sophistication. Unfortunately, one sip is all it takes.

Ummmmmm ... (quiet sputtering) no, thanks.

But there's truly nothing more picturesque than a mature vineyard. I love pouring over photos of France's wine country, *oohing* and *ahhing* at the rolling hills of carefully trained vines, greenery spilling over dusky clusters of ripening grapes. The images are richly pastoral, calling to mind pictures of sun-browned laborers bending in the heat and galas celebrating fruitful harvests.

Abundance.

When the Lord declares in Hosea 2:15 that the wilderness is His location of choice for presenting His bride with the gift of a vineyard, our spiritual skepticism can get triggered. To the casual observer, the desert seems to be the least likely place for cultivating a lush plantation.

Although the dry, alkaline soil of the wilderness provides protection from agricultural pests and diseases, it can also cause vine dehydration. Grape vines are fairly hearty, but like any plant, they must have water to grow. Without adequate rainfall or irrigation, a vineyard won't survive, let alone produce an abundant harvest.

In spite of that biological reality, the Lord uses the real-life imagery of thriving vineyards throughout scripture to mark significant physical and spiritual transitions for His people. Beginning in the book of Genesis with the post-flood narrative of Noah and running all the way to the book of Amos, the burgundy-rich thread of Old Testament vineyards weaves a picture of spiritual shifting: from slavery to freedom. From hardship to favor. From destruction to restoration.

So, when the Lord promises that He's gifting His beloved with a wilderness vineyard, those of us who have sojourned for any stint in the desert should pay attention.

KINGDOM VINEYARDS

God's first Old Testament mention of a vineyard specifically connected with His kids' hearts is found in Isaiah 5. The Lord compares the nation of Israel to His vineyard, saying *"For the vineyard of the Lord of hosts is the house of Israel, and the men of Judah are His pleasant planting..." (v. 7a)*.

For those of us made alive in Jesus through the New Covenant, we have been grafted into the "vineyard" of the children of Israel *(Romans 9-11)*. When the Lord refers to Jacob's offspring as a field of grapevines, we can activate our sanctified imagination, picturing ourselves as a part of that agricultural metaphor, taking to heart the same message which Isaiah delivered to God's people.

The prophet describes how the Lord looks for the vines of the hearts of Israel to bear richly cultivated grapes, but they come up wild instead.

My take-away?

Because Jesus compares my life to a vineyard, ripe with the richest of fruit, I need to intentionally check the condition of my heart's soil. Is it soft and fertile, ready to receive God's word planted deeply? Is it acidic with bitterness, unforgiveness, doubt, or fear, causing the grapes to spoil? Are there weeds, rocks, or thorns of unrepentant sin present that would choke the life out of my Kingdom harvest?

Unfortunately, the ancient Israelites didn't heed the prophet's warning. As a result, they experienced the consequences of their hardened hearts: physical captivity and the destruction of their homes and cities.

Hundreds of years later, the Messiah steps onto the scene.

As Jesus ministers throughout the territories of Rome-occupied Galilee and Judea, he reintroduces the metaphor of Israel as a vineyard. In Matthew 21:33-46, he verbally paints a picture of a vineyard which is leased to evil tenants who choose to hoard the harvest, reject His messengers, and eventually, murder His only Son. This not-so-subtle prophetic indictment of the religious leaders of Jesus' day infuriates them.

He then expands His vineyard comparison beyond even His disciples' comprehension. In Matthew 20:1-16, Jesus likens the Kingdom of Heaven to the master of a house who goes out early in the morning to hire laborers for His vineyard. Throughout the course of the "day," he brings on fresh workers, promising them an identical wage for their differing stints of toil.

With the use of these two metaphors, Jesus upends the religious paradigms of His fellow Jews. He introduces a

Kingdom that expands far beyond the geopolitical borders of Israel or even the bloodline of Abraham. It's a Kingdom based not on position, worth, or works but instead on calling, obedience, and grace.

My New Covenant heartcheck needs to include Jesus' vineyard descriptions. Is there any place in my soul that embraces a bitter or religious spirit, criticizing God's works or His ways? Have I judged God as guilty because He hasn't acted in the manner I expected? Have I rejected His voice or His commands, embracing instead my own ideas of what is best for my life, unwilling to trust His timing or His purpose?

To get the full picture of where we're headed, we need to examine one final, seemingly unconnected parable:

> *"The kingdom of heaven is like treasure hidden in a field, which a man found and covered up. Then in his joy he goes and sells all that he has and buys that field."*
> Matthew 13:44

I love how Jesus paints such a vivid word picture. What would it feel like to stumble upon a priceless treasure in an open field? If I didn't have the ready money, wouldn't I explore every possible option just to purchase that piece of land? Jesus understands how we're wired, so He knows exactly how to describe the incomparable worth of the Kingdom. Hidden treasure has always been an irresistible lure for the human heart.

As I examine my heart in relation to this final parable, I have to understand that this spiritual territory containing the Kingdom of God is worth everything I have. Have I been willing to exchange all that I prize most in this world order to "buy" that field? Have I counted it to be worth the cost?

THE FRUIT OF WISDOM

Before we continue, let's take a quick turn back to the book of Proverbs. Many of us are familiar with the author's description found in chapter 31 of the godly woman, otherwise known as the excellent wife. I want us to focus specifically on verse 16.

> *"She considers a field and buys it; from her profits she plants a vineyard."*

The virtuous woman is industrious. She's creative, merciful, and compassionate. She's also savvy. She knows how to spot a venture of legitimate worth. She understands a smart investment, and she's wise enough to maximize her profits through an increased return. Once she has scoped out available land, carefully weighing her risk and opportunity, she then buys a field. After watching the market and waiting for the right timing, she uses her profits and *plants a vineyard*.

Sound familiar?

Any reputable wealth manager will tell you that an investor who becomes jaded can miss the critical moment for financial breakthrough. Doubt and uncertainty can cause a person to lock their pocketbook down tight, unwilling to take the risk that can yield tremendous increase.

When Jesus woos you, His cherished bride, into the wilderness, you already hold the deed for the most priceless treasure this world will ever know. The Kingdom of Heaven is yours, lock, stock, and barrel. Moth and rust can't destroy it. Thieves can't break in to steal. You gave your life to gain it, and the return on your investment is breathtaking.

But the journey through that dry dust can do things to your heart. When you question the worth of your life's investment because the going is tough, spiritual callouses build up. When you pull inward to self-protect from fear, pain, and disappointment, you can close out the whispers of the Spirit, even His very preparation for your transition into abundance. And when you shut down your heart due to the weariness of lugging the burden of unbelief, you can miss it—the moment when Jesus places the key to your vineyard abundance in your hand.

The wise woman sees. She looks past the temporary setbacks, the possible losses, and the disappointing ventures. She holds tight to her territory, believing with a Spirit-birthed tenacity that her *kairos* moment is coming, *the God-ordained, opportune time* to leverage her original investment and cultivate a vineyard—her place of Kingdom harvest.

OUR KINSMAN-REDEEMER

One of my favorite names for Christ is *kinsman-redeemer*. Outlined by God in the law of Moses, the *goel* was required to redeem family property that had been lost through mismanagement or extenuating circumstances (Leviticus 25:23-28). In the case of a wife whose husband had left her widowed, the *goel* would purchase her as his bride, carrying on the name of the family member who had died. In either case, the kinsman-redeemer had to be willing to pay the price of redemption.

The book of Ruth illustrates the role of the *goel* so poignantly. Ruth, a widowed Moabite, along with her widowed mother-in-law Naomi, travels to Naomi's homeland to seek a new life. It's there in Bethlehem that Naomi avails herself of her family's kinsman-redeemer, Boaz. With humility and compassion, that prosperous landowner steps into the gap to restore to Naomi the property that her husband had forfeited when he migrated to Moab. In the process, Boaz gains Ruth as his bride.

This is our Jesus.

He is our kinsman-redeemer, the One who restores to us the land that has been made desolate, barren, and unfruitful. He buys back our inheritance through His own blood, handing the purchase deed back into our keeping. And then He does what no one else can. He steps into the desolate wilderness of our lives, unkept and uncultivated, and He transforms it. Irrigating it with the water of His Spirit, He pours down abundance. Before we can even realize what is happening, a vineyard sprouts right before our eyes.

In His last hours before the cross, Christ's role as kinsman-redeemer was likely at the forefront of His mind. As Jesus and His disciples partake in a final Passover meal together, He shares His heart with those who will soon become His cherished bride. Opening up the mystery of the vineyard, He explains the beauty of New Covenant bounty:

> *"I am the vine; you are the branches. Whoever abides in me and I in him, he it is that bears much fruit, for apart from me you can do nothing."*
>
> John 15:5

No longer does He describe Israel as a fruitless vineyard. Instead, He inserts Himself into the narrative as the source of all fruitfulness. Jesus Himself is our true vine. As His beloved, we become living extensions of who He is. We are the branches, with His lifeblood coursing through us and His rootedness causing us to flourish.

When we abide in Him, allowing ourselves to be made one with Him through the great bridal mystery that is the Church, we bear much fruit.

He's such a lavish lover. As our Bridegroom bestows upon His bride His wedding gift of a vineyard, the dust of our desert begins to bloom. The grapes swell round and crisp, carrying a liquid more heady than any that man can contrive. It's the power of the Spirit, filling every leaking crevice of our souls.

Abundant fruit. A celebratory harvest.

And the best part? There's no bitter burning to gulp down. This fruit of His vine is sweeter than honey.

100 FOLD FRUIT

In 2016, the Lord called our family to a stint of living in Costa Rica. Within my first few weeks of living in the jungle on the Pacific coast, I had penned these words.

> The passion of Jesus is too great; He's too jealous a lover to allow me to continue to just exist, comfortable in my status quo. So He allows me to be exposed to pain, challenge, hurt, and I startle awake, pulsing with an awareness that there is so much more.
>
> Because there is always so much more in Him.
>
> My comfort challenged, I realize that splendor has been waiting just below the surface of my determined reach for ease. Not all of us are called to pull up and move to a foreign mission field for the long term. *But every one of us is called to really live.*
>
> So we abandon our props, our soul sedatives, and we come awake.
>
> Wide awake to pain and beauty.
>
> Wide awake to the challenge and glory that is *abundant life*.[1]

As the Lord intentionally challenged my notions of comfort and abundance, I was hungrily reaching for a deeper experience with Him. Right in the middle of that space, He showed up.

One morning as I was sitting in the jungle-quiet with Him, Jesus whispered, **"Ask me to make you into a 100-fold woman."** I had always assumed that it was the Father who chose the measure of my fruit, already determining in advance how plentiful my Kingdom harvest would be. And like a good daddy, when He saw that I just didn't get what He was saying, He repeated the instruction.

"Ask me to make you into a 100-fold woman."

Because I had been studying the parable of the sower, I eventually caught His meaning. *"And other seeds fell into good soil and produced grain, growing up and increasing and yielding thirtyfold and sixtyfold and a hundredfold"* (Mark 4:20). So, in spite of my fear that I was somehow being heretical, I started asking.

Father, I want to bear more fruit in your Kingdom. I don't want to settle for 30 or 60 fold. I'm boldly asking you for a 100-fold return on Your investment. Let the seeds that You've sown in my life explode with abundance.

Ever since that season, He keeps reminding me that it's His Word and His Spirit which cause my life to bear fruit. When His Word abides in me, the power of His Spirit fuses with the beauty of my obedience, and something of eternal value is borne. I just have to stay connected to Him, deeply intimate with His heart. As I do, a fragrance rises from my life that draws those around me to notice the stunningness of Christ.

But that beauty and fragrance, they're only the beginning. Because those are just outward markers. Deep down, real fruit is developing.

WILDERNESS ABUNDANCE

In light of Jesus' teaching and parables, a good friend recently posed a question which sprung from her desert challenges. *"Do you believe every Christian has to go through the wilderness?"*

In other words, *does all abundant fruitfulness originate from the pruning of a wilderness season?*

And because hearts that are traveling through the wasteland are fragile treasures, I chewed carefully on her query before responding.

Yes, I do.

But can I qualify that?

I firmly believe that the Word of God demonstrates that if your heart beats for Jesus—if you hunger and thirst for more of Him and pant for His presence like a deer pants for the water brooks— He *will* lead you into the desert.

If you want to look like Jesus, carrying His glory and releasing His Kingdom everywhere you go, He *will* guide you into the wasteland.

If you want to see His face, touch His heart, and hear His voice more than ever before—more than you even believe is possible—He *will* escort you into the wilderness.

And throughout Scripture, this truth is painted in vivid color:

The wilderness is the pathway to promotion.

Everything of eternity which our spirits were created to hold.

Everything we long to taste, see, and carry.

The *more* of Jesus and His Kingdom.

All of this is uncovered in the desert.

Because abundant fruitfulness is the Father's aim for your life, He loves you too much to allow any hindrances to that glory to remain rooted in your soul. So, Jesus woos you into the wilderness. He draws you with His rich *chesed* and tenderly takes your hand, carefully surveying the desolate places in your heart. As you lean into His love, allowing Him to completely tear down the walls which divide your heart from His, He regenerates your life, rebuilding the ruins of brokenness. But He doesn't leave you there.

David declares in Psalm 23:4b-5, *"Your rod and your staff, they comfort me. You prepare a table before me in the presence of my enemies; you anoint my head with oil; my cup overflows."*

The beautiful rebuilding of Jesus always leads to a fresh feasting at the His table. Through the remembrance of His sacrifice, you savor the bread and the wine, dining on His body and His blood *(1 Corinthians 11:23-26)*. Celebration and dancing break out. Soul-songs explode, borne of the freedom of being fully known, fully loved. Anointing flows fresh, spilling over in an unending flow of the Spirit. And you receive the bridal gift of your vineyard, all burgeoning with blossoms.

The apostle Paul explains it this way:

> *"Therefore, since we have been justified by faith, we have peace with God through our Lord Jesus Christ. Through him we have also obtained access by faith into this grace in which we stand, and we rejoice in hope of the glory of God. Not only that, but we rejoice in our sufferings, knowing that suffering produces endurance, and endurance produces character, and character produces hope, and hope does*

not put us to shame, because God's love has been poured into our hearts through the Holy Spirit who has been given to us."
Romans 5:1-5

The gate of your vineyard is swinging wide, leading you straight onto a path towards the door of hope.

Beloved, it is time to reap a harvest of joy. Joy is your inheritance, and nothing can stand in its path. My joy is your true strength. Let that joy rise within you, overcoming every obstacle.

You were created to achieve great things, to bring immense glory to My name. Cast away every fear that holds you back and run. Run into the light of My countenance, which is the joy I experience every time I look at you, my dear one.

Celebrate the abundant harvest I am placing into your hands. It will exceed what your hands can hold, more than you believe you deserve. This is the season. This is the time. Seize the tremendous goodness I have stored up for you and step into the dance with Me.

1. Tiffany Nesbitt, 2016, March 23. Turning the Corner. Streamroots. https://streamroots.com/posts/turning-the-corner/

FIVE
a door of hope

> "Sharon will become a pasture for flocks, and the Valley of Achor a resting place for herds for my people who seek me."
>
> *Isaiah 65:10*

SOMETIMES EXPERIENCING the transformation of hope requires us to first make a trek deep into the wilderness.

Having returned to Southern California from a four-year season in Nashville, our family experienced one challenge after another as we struggled to find a sense of spiritual and practical footing. While we prayed, fasted, and sought the Lord for direction, we moved from one temporary haven to the next, lugging our suitcases and crates of homeschool books with us. Eventually, friends from church provided a renovated cottage for us to rent at a reduced rate. With all of our possessions still stored in PODS in a Tennessee warehouse, we scrambled to gather enough furnishings to fill the 800-square-foot home for our family of six. Tiny as it was, that cottage provided a desperately needed anchor of stability in the midst of an ongoing Job-like season.

But in spite of finally having a place to call home, my heart was deeply wrestling.

I was asking questions, and Jesus wasn't answering. It wasn't that He was silent. It was just that His communication felt far too concise and vague.

Trust Me. Don't be afraid. Hope in Me.

His words repeated like a scratched vinyl album, continually bumping against the same worn-out lyrics. And what He was saying didn't satisfy my deep groaning to understand *why*. When I would press for more, I would hear nothing but silence.

Three years later, I was asked to speak at a women's Christmas tea. It was my first opportunity for public ministry since returning to California, and I was undeniably nervous. Since God hadn't been talking to me on a deeply personal level, how could I be confident that He would give me anything impactful to share corporately? For weeks, I dove into preparation with an intensity born of desperation.

Come on, Jesus. Please, give me something.

About one week before my speaking date, the Holy Spirit unexpectedly took me to Isaiah 54:1-3:

> *"'Sing, O barren one, who did not bear; break forth into singing and cry aloud, you who have not been in labor! For the children of the desolate one will be more than the children of her who is married,' says the Lord. 'Enlarge the place of your tent, and let the curtains of your habitations be stretched out; do not hold back; lengthen your cords and strengthen your stakes. For you will spread abroad to the right and to the left, and your offspring will possess the nations and will people the desolate cities.'"*

Bam.

In a suddenness that was breathtaking, the Spirit downloaded truth like Niagara roaring in its spring thaw.

With the closing message of the book of Malachi, the Lord of Israel seems to seal up the heavens. Just as with the close of the Old Testament period of the Judges, God's chosen people walk through a season in which *"...the word of the Lord was rare in those days; there was no frequent vision"* (1 Samuel 3:1b).

So they wait. Through war, invasion, and occupation, they wait. Through revolutionary uprisings and the sullen quiet of peace, they wait. And they wither. The ground of their hearts grows hard, crusted over by the barrenness of too many generations. They wait for the breakthrough of promise, for the deliverance of the Messiah. They wait for the reminder that Yahweh's eternal covenant has not been forgotten and that fruit can once again be borne in their desert land.

FROM BARREN TO BIRTHING

As I studied, the Lord reminded me that this period of Jewish history was reminiscent of the life of Sarah, the barren wife of the patriarch Abraham. Thousands of years earlier, she had laughed without mirth because her hardened heart couldn't receive the joy of God's birthing declaration.

He also directed my attention to the pain of Hannah, the mother of the prophet Samuel. Before the birth of her firstborn, she had wept in hopelessness because her years of barrenness seemed to be unalterable proof of God's abandonment.

But just as in the lives of Sarah and Hannah, during Israel's 400 fallow years, the Father was working—preparing for the planned-from-the-beginning-of-time moment when He would shout and shatter the silence. And when He did, it was the barren place that would become the incubator of life.

In a shockingly unexpected encounter recorded in Luke 1, the angel Gabriel declares to Zechariah the priest that his childless wife, Elizabeth, will bear a son—the very one who will fulfill the final prophecy of the book of Malachi. And in Zechariah's astonished response, the hidden cache of his heart is exposed: unbelief.

It's been too long, Lord. Too much sojourning in this lifeless wasteland. Too much pain and silence.

Zechariah embodies the spirit of his generation, embracing a posture of heart-hardened, wilderness-wandering unbelief.

Don't we often find ourselves in the company of Sarah, Hannah, and Zechariah—in the place where *we* are the waiting ones whose barrenness can seem too much to endure? And when our longing for redemption is continually delayed, hope withers and we shrivel into unbelief.

But the best parts of our story, of *every* story, start with God-breathed, divine declarations. Our God who declares, **"Let there be Light!"** is the same God who stoops to breathe the *ruah*, the *Spirit-wind of life*, into our hearts. And just as in Isaiah 54, Jesus declares to our barren places:

Sing. Cry Aloud. Stretch forth. Make ready! Redemption is about to overwhelm this parched land like a flood. Lengthen your cords! Strengthen your stakes!

Israel's ancient nomads would have easily grasped the metaphor. Their tents, patched together with pieces of goats' skins, were often stretched to contain the blessing of new life or increased possessions. The cords were then lengthened to hold in place the expanded skins. The stakes, firmly hammered to anchor the enlarged dwelling, were secured.

CORDS OF HOPE

Although the Hebrew word used for *cords* in Isaiah 54:3 carries the specific meaning of strings, the Lord showed me that Joshua 2 uses a second, powerful word to convey the idea of a cord.

At the front end of the Canaanite conquest, two Israelite spies promise to deliver the prostitute Rahab and her family from the coming destruction of Jericho, instructing her to hang a scarlet cord from her window. Verse 21 describes Rahab's lifeline as a *tiqvah,* a derivative of the Hebrew word *qavah,* meaning *hope, expectation, or the thing longed for.*

Cords of hope.

Through the prophet Isaiah, God announces to His children that their season of hopelessness is over. It's time to catch hold of hope like a lifeline and stretch it out, moving forward. He declares that those who have wandered in a barren land must now enlarge their scope, trusting the proclamations He is singing over them, fully convinced that His promises never disappoint.

And those sinewy cords must be anchored to stakes of faith.

It is faith that gives hope its resiliency, its tenacity. Without those stalwart stakes, hope is lost, and the home of our hearts is placed in jeopardy.

Through the prophet's ancient words, the Lord makes a declaration over our hearts:

It's time to believe.

Time to pound into the ground the anchors which will not give way in the shifting sands of the desert, strengthening our faith. It's time to preach to our souls and to challenge them, *"Be strong and very courageous" (Joshua 1:9).*

In the New Testament, the Greek word which is most often translated as hope is *elpís*, meaning *that in which one confides or to which he flees for refuge; expectation of what is sure; to anticipate or welcome.* Paul uses this word in a compelling demonstration of the need for hope wrapped around faith, stating in Hebrews 11:1, *"Now faith is the assurance of things hoped for..."*

And again in Romans 4:18 & 20, *"In hope* (Abraham)

believed against hope, that he should become the father of many nations, as he had been told, 'So shall your offspring be... No unbelief made (Abraham) *waver concerning the promise of God, but he grew strong in his faith as he gave glory to God, fully convinced that God was able to do what he had promised."*

Abraham hoped in God's promise, so he believed.

The act of stretching out our cords, of strengthening our stakes — it's an act of hope wrapped around faith. It's a powerful declaration in the face of the enemy and every opposing circumstance that our God is a covenant-keeping, promise-fulfilling Father.

And there's more.

When we surrender to salvation, the Holy Spirit initiates the next leg of our God-ordained journey. Based on a course that was mapped out before the foundation of the world, He leads us toward all the sanctification and good works that He has prepared for us to walk in *(Ephesians 2:10)*.

But here's the clincher: even before salvation, our Trail Guide has plans to woo us into the desert. If we were privileged to catch a heavenly bird's-eye view of our life's path, we would find several wasteland stints already colored into the landscape. Jesus' burning desire is not only to bring us into blissful union with Him as

His pure and spotless bride, but He also longs for us to fully apprehend every spiritual blessing which has been given to us in the heavenlies *(Ephesians 1:3)*, walking in the abundance of our divine call and releasing His Kingdom on the earth.

A MINDSET SHIFT

To fully understand this, we need to examine the course which the Father charted for His kids when He delivered them from Egypt. Many Old Testament scholars teach that the journey from the Egyptian region of Goshen, where the Israelites lived as slaves, to the Promised Land of Canaan was a less than two-week trip. Why, then, did God direct them through such a circuitous desert wandering? Aside from the additional forty years tacked onto their travel due to unbelief, Exodus 13:17-18 provides an explanation:

> *"When Pharaoh let the people go, God did not lead them by way of the land of the Philistines, although that was near. For God said, 'Lest the people change their minds when they see war and return to Egypt.' But God led the people around by the way of the wilderness toward the Red Sea. And the people of Israel went up out of the land of Egypt equipped for battle."*

After hundreds of years of enslavement, the Israelites had one mindset: bondage. They thought, worked, ate, slept, played, and rested as slaves. But in order for them to step into the fulfillment of their promise, they had to be transformed into a company of warriors. Their old ways of thinking had to crumble, supernaturally transformed into that of faith-filled strategists and legendary heroes who would conquer and steward a bountiful land, proclaiming the glory of Yahweh throughout the earth.

Because of the way in which our brains and hearts are wired, the intense stretch of a complete paradigm shift takes time. Implicit trust requires relational history and proven dependability. So, the Lord leads the Israelites by way of the Sinai, allowing them the opportunity to embrace the necessary transformation.

But God's promise in Genesis 15:7 provides proof that abundance was always the destination of the children of Abraham, *"And he said to him, 'I am the Lord who brought you out from Ur of the Chaldeans to give you this land to possess."* Before Israel ever traveled down into Egypt, the Father had purposed to give His people a plentiful territory marked by increase and overflow.

When we step into the wilderness, we find ourselves right in the middle of the God-ordained path to our promise. However, in order for us to hold the increase of all that impending goodness, our mindsets have to shift. Our capacity has to expand. We need to stretch far beyond our natural capabilities, yielding instead to His supernatural ability. This intentional stretching process can often overwhelm our spiritual senses, leaving us feeling only the pain of the pull. Nevertheless, when we partner with His process through intentional submission, obedience, and risk, we are positioned for a breakthrough in the wilderness. Before we realize it, hope is blossoming, and we are walking into the territory that has been prepared for us all along: a place of increased stewardship, Kingdom authority, and Holy Spirit anointing.

OUR WILDERNESS FORERUNNER

Our Savior Himself carved this path for us to follow. Luke relates that immediately following His baptism, the Holy Spirit led Jesus into the wilderness, where he fasted for forty days and was tempted by the devil *(Luke 4:1-2)*.

The Gospel accounts of Jesus' desert journey leave me with some musings:

Did Jesus know where the Holy Spirit was leading Him?

Did He have prophetic insight that His ministry would launch on the other side of the desert?

Was He prepared for the harsh reality of a challenging fast and unprecedented satanic temptation?

In spite of those unanswered questions, one thing is clear: Christ's surrendered embrace of His wilderness experience prepared and propelled Him into His eternal purpose. As the precursor to His climb to Calvary, Jesus' sinless navigation of His time in the desert provides a road-map for my own wasteland experience. It's the upside-down way of the Kingdom: challenge, lack, and isolation expand me to carry an uncontainable measure of heavenly favor, abundance, and blessing.

This truth is the bedrock of our hope.

SINGING INTO BREAKTHROUGH

Isaiah 54 pushes us one step further. As we move forward, expanding our territory, we are called to *sing*. To cry aloud in praise. That physical activation of our faith releases a take-notice chorus to every spiritual force in the heavenly places that we are a people who will not wither in hopelessness. Instead, we will stand and watch our God transform every place of barrenness into triumph.

Preparing for that Christmas message shifted something deep within me. For seven years, I had foolishly assumed that as I waited for the Lord to lead me out of my desert season, He expected me to posture myself in a pitiful combination of passive resignation and grit-my-teeth superhuman endurance.

With that Isaiah 54 revelation, the Lord revealed that He longed for a different kind of partnership with me. He was inviting me to press into the breath of His Spirit and sing—out loud—right in the middle of my barren place. To cry out that the King of the Universe was about to do me good. He was urging me to yank those quivering stakes of faith up from the wilderness floor, stretch out my shriveled cords of hope—far beyond what I thought was their snapping point—and take new territory in the Spirit.

Because I hungered for the breakthrough, I took a deep breath and tried my darndest to sing. I tried to lengthen cords and hammer stakes. But after seven years of disappointments and delays, even the thought of trying to hope felt like banging my head against an immovable stone wall. It hurt way too much.

I was terrified of being disappointed again, of experiencing shame and discouragement as a result of another defeat and no breakthrough. Instead of stretching and pounding, I stood quaking in my spiritual boots, frozen in fear.

That's when the Holy Spirit began to whisper to me from Hosea chapter two. As He did, it was verse fifteen that captivated me the most.

> *"...and (I will) make the valley of Achor into a door of hope."*

I was beyond desperate for hope, and my curiosity was piqued. Why did the Lord declare that He would transform that particular valley into the kind of passageway I was longing for?

I found the answer in Joshua 8.

A DOOR OF HOPE

Within days of Israel's miraculous defeat of the city of Jericho, right in the middle of apprehending their centuries-old promise of conquering the land of milk and honey, the people of God come to a screeching halt. With victory shouts still fresh on their lips, they advance to attack the relatively unprotected city of Ai. However, instead of an easy victory, Israel's armies experience a demoralizing slaughter.

In the aftermath of their defeat, Joshua stumbles into the tent of meeting, the dust of defeat covering his head and his shredded clothes. God responds to his cry, revealing to Israel's leader that sin has infected the camp. Under the cover of Jericho's demolition, one man had snatched some of the city's spoil, treasure that the Lord had instructed Israel to destroy completely as an offering unto Himself. Tucked under Achan's tent, those stolen goods had cried out from the ground against the entirety of God's people.

As the grieving and bewildered nation assembles, the Lord highlights the guilty clan: the family of Achan. Achan confesses his covetousness, and God's righteous consequences are delivered. According to the instruction of the Lord, Joshua responds:

> *"And Joshua and all Israel with him took Achan the son of Zerah, and the silver and the cloak and the bar of gold, and his sons and daughters and his oxen and donkeys and sheep and his tent and all that he had. And they brought them up to the Valley of Achor. And Joshua said, 'Why did you bring trouble on us? The Lord brings trouble on you today.' And all Israel stoned him with stones. They burned them with fire and stoned them with stones. And they raised over him a great heap of stones that remains to this day. Then the Lord turned from his burning anger. Therefore, to this day the name of that place is called the Valley of Achor."*
> Joshua 7:24-26

The word *Achor* sounds like the Hebrew word for *trouble*;

Joshua rightly indicts Achan with bringing *trouble* upon an entire nation. With the execution of Achan's family, the whole people of Israel are marked by an experience of shame, a testifying heap of stones standing as a reminder of sin and defeat.

Like those Israelites, we can be easily convinced that our past will forever dictate our future. That we will never achieve true victory and conquer our promised land. That we've been disqualified by hidden sin which trips us up and lays us flat, leaving us buried under heaps of stony condemnation.

In light of Joshua's story, I went back and mulled over Hosea's redemption declaration. The very vale where the traitor, Achan, had caused an entire nation to be routed is the spot where God declares that He will craft a doorway of hope. As I pondered and processed, I began to grasp an amazing truth:

It's the very dust of our defeats, the pain from our past, which the Lord uses to create a door of hope, all brand new and flung wide open.

It didn't end well for Achan or his family. It was messy and grievous. More than hard. The Israelites experienced up close and personal how highly God values obedience and how tightly it ties to victory. It was a bit of national history which most Jews would have likely preferred to sweep briskly under their tent flaps, leaving the pain buried beneath layers of desert dust.

But that's not the end of the story—not for the Jewish nation or for us.

OUR TRUE HOPE

Over the past decades, I've noticed a disturbing trend. I've watched as believers in Jesus—strong, beautiful women—have wrestled through devastating wilderness seasons. In the process of trying to make sense of the impact of the sin of others which has shattered their lives and dreams or of their own disappointment with God, their faith morphs. The destruction of everything they once held dear instigates a rebellious pursuit of "finding themselves." At some point in that journey, they question everything. What once was bedrock is replaced by shifting sand.

Life hasn't worked out the way it was supposed to. Relationships have caused more hurt than happiness. Motherhood has been more self-sacrificing than fulfilling. Careers haven't succeeded. Dreams have died. And the past just won't stay in the past.

As a result, universalism, syncretism, feminism, hedonism—almost anything goes for these dear ones who have lost their way. Fingers get pointed at the Church, their families, and friends. Victim flags get waved. "I deserve my best life" becomes their battle cry.

Suddenly, the woman I once knew no longer exists. She has been replaced by a version 2.0 of herself—except this model has too many bugs and glitches to run smoothly. Instead of being the upgrade it's pitched to be, it's a recipe for self-destruction. In actuality, it's a masterful rip-off by the enemy, robbing these dear ones of their Kingdom identity, stealing their joy and peace, and deceiving them into believing they're far more enlightened and better off that way.

Many of these women openly share their stories on social media, preaching that they're a stronger adaptation of themselves. Through a self-concocted recipe—a pinch of Jesus, a cupful of humanism, and a strong dash of follow-your-heart ideology—they claim to have discovered an untamed strength, made all the tastier by its wild independence. Instead, they're trapped. Like the children of Israel who chose fear, complaint, and doubt over faith when faced with their giants, they've doomed themselves to wander in the wilderness until they drop in the dirt. Each time their journey leads them near that pile of stones covering past failures, the hurt rises quickly, and their hearts short-circuit a bit more. The healing they are searching everywhere to find is elusive; heartache etches their faces. And because their new life often includes a rejection of anything or anyone labeled as "judging," even the truth told in love can't be borne.

This should ignite a righteous anger in our souls—anger against the enemy's tactics and the way he succeeds over and over again. It should also deeply grieve us. The collateral damage of such a painful progression of choices is multi-generational, with its consequences reaching farther than we can comprehend, affecting not only families and churches, but the culture of an entire nation.

To claim simply that "Jesus is the answer" can feel like blithely quoting an outdated Sunday school lesson to a Harvard philosophy professor. However, the truth is that simple: Jesus *is* the answer. He is the beginning and the end of our healing process. Self-realization, self-reliance, and being "true to ourselves" are nothing but band-aids on festering wounds. Jesus alone is the healer.

These self-made monuments to our poor decisions or outright failures can often clutter the floor of our wilderness. Pesky pebbles and stones get caught in our shoes, continually bruising our souls. The larger boulders are often used to construct our walls of self-defeat, isolation, and protectionism, separating us from our Promised Land abundance.

But God's redemption is absolutely transformational.

ANCHORED IN HOPE

Beloved, when we choose to anchor ourselves to hope in Jesus, right in the face of our unanswered questions, unexplained pain, or deepest shame, something miraculous takes place. The Lover of our soul changes those standing stones into something so captivating that our hearts ache with its beauty and glory. His plan for our good is so far-reaching that our minds can't begin to grasp its magnitude.

Bending down, He thoughtfully scoops a grainy pile of pebbles. Carefully, He breathes. And right before our eyes, an opening forms in the wall ahead of us, wide and clear.

Stones of shame transformed to an archway of blessing.

A door of hope.

> "Oh give thanks to the Lord, for he is good, for his steadfast love endures forever! Let the redeemed of the Lord say so, whom he has redeemed from trouble and gathered in from the lands, from the east and from the west, from the north and from the south. Some wandered in desert wastes, finding no way to a city to dwell in; hungry and thirsty, their soul fainted within them. Then they cried to the Lord in their trouble, and he delivered them from their distress. He led them by a straight way till they

reached a city to dwell in. Let them thank the Lord for his steadfast love, for his wondrous works to the children of man! For he satisfies the longing soul, and the hungry soul he fills with good things."
Psalm 107:1-9

"For I know the plans I have for you, declares the Lord, plans for welfare and not for evil, to give you a future and a hope."
Jeremiah 29:11

"May the God of hope fill you with all joy and peace in believing, so that by the power of the Holy Spirit you may abound in hope."
Romans 15:13

Beloved, you are My betrothed, and I am coming soon to bring you to Myself. Do not throw away your confidence, which has a great reward. Strengthen your cord of hope—it is My anchor for your soul. Walk in strong assurance.

Rest in My heart for you without striving. Lean into My love and be still, knowing that I alone am God. Only I hold your world in My hands. Not a hair of your

head falls to the ground apart from Me. Not a breath fills your lungs without My word going forth to hold you together. I am that close, that near. I am God, and there is no other.

I am quickly bringing things to completion that have challenged your hope. You will stand on the other side of this mountain and see the goodness of the Lord in the land of the living. Banish doubt. Embrace hope.

How deep, how great is My love for you, My beautiful one.

SIX
your love song

> *"She will respond to me there, singing with joy as in days long ago in her youth after I had freed her from captivity in Egypt."*
>
> Hosea 2:15, The Living Bible

I'M ALWAYS delighted to watch a love story unfold. It's been my joy and privilege to walk the road of romance with quite a few spiritual daughters, listening and counseling along the way. However, out of the many stories to which I've been privy, my own daughters' romances are my favorites. Each of my girls experienced a wonderful story with the man who would become her husband. But neither of their experiences was easy. Instead, my daughters' relationships share a painful commonality, one that was tough for me to watch.

At different points in their courtships, they both rejected the men who eventually won their hearts. I've got to hand it to my sons-in-law. In spite of the heartbreak of rejection which they experienced, both of them decided to choose the course of tenacity. They individually wooed each of my daughters with a persistence and selflessness which was stunning. They kept showing up. They kept giving, serving, and listening. Each one fed the flame of hope that eventually, my daughter would respond and give him her heart. And that's exactly what happened.

For both of my girls, there was a moment when the truth of what was growing in her soul began to overtake her doubts and fears. At some point in her journey, everything changed, and she responded with an unequivocal yes to the patient, determined pursuit of that man. Love blossomed. And when it did, the joy in her life exploded. I've never seen two girls more delightedly eager to marry the very men whom they had spurned only months previously. Each in her turn was absolutely giddy—dancing around the house, singing and giggling with delight over a future that stretched out like a golden ribbon before her.

Both of their hearts were awakened by the pursuit of a deeply sacrificial love, and joy was the fruit.

LOVE'S SONG OF JOY

I have to confess to harboring some disappointment in the fact that aside from Hosea's first two acts of obedience, the biblical account doesn't record the result of his pursuit of his wayward wife. It's a reality that leaves me with a slew of questions.

How did Gomer's heart respond to Hosea's selfless love?

Did she permit his persistence to tear down her walls of resistance and pain?

Did she allow herself to thrive in his care?

And perhaps my most persistent speculation is this:

Did they ever experience joy together?

When God outlines to Hosea the path on which He is going to take His bride, He paints a powerful word picture of His goal for their divine courtship. After alluring her into the wilderness, speaking tenderly to her, presenting her with vineyards of abundance, and transforming her monuments of heartbreak into doors of hope, Jesus declares that His bride *will respond*.

She will sing for joy as in the days of her youth.

In this verse, the Lord identifies two simultaneous factors at play in His people's hearts. First, they will answer His persistent courtship with a song of total abandonment, finally choosing Him over all others. Second, they will experience a return to the time of their youth. In other words, they'll flourish again because of their wildly powerful joy.

CULTIVATING JOY

My husband and I have recently been studying the function of joy in the brain and how it affects the development of Christian character and community. Most of us have been taught that the right side of our brain controls creativity and emotion, while the left side processes logic and reason. Although this generalization is rooted in truth, scientists have uncovered additional facts about how the hemispheres of our brain operate in tandem to govern relational interactions and accomplish our sanctification process.

Every piece of neurological stimulus begins its processing journey in the right side of our brain. Information enters at the back of the right hemisphere where we begin to analyze it subconsciously, then moves to the front of our brain and crosses into the left hemisphere, where we attach words to our initial impressions. This transit happens much faster than conscious thought. In fact, the right side of the brain processes incoming stimulus at six times per second, much faster than the left side. And because the right side of the brain governs the majority of our relational attachments, emotional responses, and character formation, our right hemisphere is drawing conclusions that impact our choices and relationships before the left hemisphere can even form words to define those choices.

But our biggest discovery has been the fact that joy is one of the most powerful shapers of our brain's right hemisphere.

Joy has such a profound effect that neuroscientists have postulated that the right hemisphere actually runs at the speed of joy, while our left hemisphere runs at the speed of words.

Additionally, scientists have stated that when we make extended direct eye contact with another human, our right-brain joy receptors are stimulated. Without conscious awareness, endorphins are released, and joy rises. As a result, our relational attachment to that person deepens, and we feel a heightened sense of connectedness and well-being[1].

In other words, healthy intimacy produces joy.

TESTIMONY OF JOY

How does all of this correlate to the story of Hosea and our wilderness journeys? Think about it this way. Just before Jesus climbs the hill to Golgotha, He imparts transformational truth which He knows will sustain His disciples through the disillusionment of His crucifixion.

John records Jesus' words in chapter 15, verses 10-11, *"If you keep my commandments, you will abide in my love, just as I have kept my Father's commandments and abide in his love. These things I have spoken to you that my joy may be in you and your joy may be full."*

Jesus outlines the crucial correlation between obedience, love, and joy. He explains that when His disciples obey Him, they abide in His love. In other words, their intimacy with His heart increases. As a result, their joy rises to its fullest capacity.

Beloved, this is what your wilderness is designed to accomplish.

Through His tender love and infinite wisdom, Jesus allures us into our desert seasons. He invites us to gaze deep into His eyes, reminding us of His heart and calling us back to true obedience—what it means to follow Him no matter the cost. In that barren place where all we can offer is our *yes*, each step forward increases our intimacy with Him. We encounter His presence in ways we've never before experienced. And our love for Him begins to rise. He reminds us of our history with Him, highlighting the time when our hearts exploded with a joy so potent that we could hardly contain it—when all we could think about was Jesus. We remember what it feels like to be crazy in love. Before we can analyze it with words, joy is coursing through our veins so powerfully that we can't help but open our mouths and testify.

The Hebrew word used in Hosea 2:15 to describe Israel's response to the Lord's wooing is *anah*, which means *to sing, shout, testify, announce, and respond.* God explains to Hosea that His people will respond to His courtship with an explosion of joy. They will sing, shout, and testify with an utter delight that matches the exuberance which they demonstrated when they came out of Egypt.

In order to really grasp what this looks like, we need to jump back to the Exodus account of Israel's deliverance from Pharaoh's army. Many of us are familiar with the story of how God miraculously delivered His people from slavery. After bringing ruinous plagues upon the people of Egypt, God leads the Israelites to the edge of the Red Sea. Trapped between the water and Pharoah's pursuing armies, His people desperately cry for help. The Lord responds by miraculously creating a dry path through the deep. Once Israel's millions have crossed, the waters supernaturally return to their place, and Pharaoh's army is drowned. It's a stunning moment in Israel's story, one which solidly defines their corporate identity as Yahweh's beloved people.

Exodus 15:19-21 summarizes their response:

> "*For when the horses of Pharaoh with his chariots and his horsemen went into the sea, the Lord brought back the waters of the sea upon them, but the people of Israel walked on dry ground in the midst of the sea. Then Miriam the prophetess, the sister of Aaron, took a tambourine in her hand, and all the women went out after her with tambourines and dancing. And Miriam sang to them:*
>
> *'Sing to the Lord, for he has triumphed gloriously; the horse and his rider he has thrown into the sea!'*"

Moses is also recorded as leading the entire company of Israel in song:

> "*I will sing to the Lord, for he has triumphed gloriously; the horse and his rider he has thrown into the sea. The Lord is my strength and my song, and he has become my salvation; this is my God, and I will praise him, my father's God, and I will exalt him!*"
> Exodus 15:1b-2

On the other side of their deliverance, they *sing*.

They testify to the goodness of their God. They spin, dance, and whirl with the joy of watching God undeniably prove His love. They shout about His covenantal faithfulness, responding with exhilarated gratitude.

Their worship isn't orchestrated or planned. It's the uncontrolled, spontaneous response of a company of hearts enthralled with their Beloved.

WHAT IS HOLDING BACK MY SONG?

In light of Miriam's and Moses' stunning example, I have to be willing to honestly evaluate my own heart.

If the joy of first love is my ultimate wilderness destination, what's holding back my song?

At the climax of one of my own desert seasons, the Holy Spirit led me through a series of events that caused me to evaluate my stubborn obstacles to joy. As He did, I came to a powerful realization. According to my timetable, the moment had come and gone for God to fulfill His long-delayed promises and bring my breakthrough. Because my analysis was mostly fabricated from lies of the enemy, I was wrestling with confusion, jealousy, hurt, and a fear of being forgotten. I was disappointed in God, and it ran deep.

As I recognized the ugly truth about my heart, I discovered that I had unknowingly pointed a finger of accusation against the Lord. And after days of wrestling with Jesus, I found myself teary-eyed and vulnerable, wearied from the battle to believe.

During this season, I managed to drag myself to church for a corporate worship gathering. As the leader belted out his second song, I realized the unattractive truth: my heart was rigid. I could feel the callousness deep inside me, the wrestling match between what I thought my circumstances proved and what I knew to be true. To become pliable—to be joyful again—I would have to surrender everything. But that was a white flag I wasn't willing to wave.

In that moment, the Holy Spirit spoke to me from His Word, *"Today if you hear his voice, do not harden your hearts as in the day of rebellion, on the day of testing in the wilderness where your fathers put me to the test and saw my works for forty years"* (Hebrews 3:7-9a).

Don't harden your heart, Tiffany.

My heart had become crusted over, and I wasn't sure how to fix it.

Again, the Spirit gently whispered, *"Take care, brothers, lest there be in any of you an evil, unbelieving heart, leading you to fall away from the living God"* (Hebrews 3:12).

In spite of the miracle of the Red Sea crossing and their deliverance from slavery, the Israelites hardened their hearts through unbelief. Yahweh took them into the wilderness to test them, to determine the true measure of their faith. He led them into the desert to allure them to Himself, to teach them to delight themselves in Him.

Over and over He tested them, giving them the opportunity to choose God over their fears and fleshly desires, to choose Him over all other lovers. And time and time again they chose ... *hard*. Their fear, selfishness, and pride paved the way for unbelief to take up residence in their hearts.

As I slumped in my seat, I realized that I was no different.

Unbelief had taunted: *Those promises you're clinging to are utter foolishness! Just a fantasy. Look at where belief has brought you—into the wilderness, for pity's sake! Your water is scarce, your food is rationed and dull, and the scenery is always the same ... dirt covered with scrub. To embrace hope is ridiculous.*

I was imprisoned by agreements with the enemy's lies.

In spite of myself, the Holy Spirit was oh-so-kindly making me wise to Satan's tactics. And the more clearly I evaluated my own heart, the more desperate I was to recover my joy. I knew at that moment there was only one path to freedom: complete abandonment. Abandonment of the rebellion and distrust which held me captive. Abandonment to the trustworthiness of Jesus' plans, to the goodness and the faithfulness of God.

I was confronted by the choice which He offered me: repent and believe or continue to wander with a hardened heart. I laid across a row of empty chairs and allowed the pent-up emotion to flow.

I don't want to trust when everything feels impossible! You ask too much, Jesus! I'm deep-down angry at the pain of shattered dreams. Hurt that you would let me be stripped in such an all-consuming process.

My anger raged in an unchecked stream of tears.

Right in the middle of my unholy mess, the unexpected happened. The crust around my heart began to crumble, tenderly chiseled by the Master Potter. I could feel it shattering in chunks, my defenses useless. My heart lay naked before Him, pulsing with the emotional baggage of the previous eight years; in spite of the pain, He was giving me the grace to embrace the wild work of God, melting my stony soul.

By the last song, I was crumpling mountains of soggy Kleenex and pushing myself to stand. And for the first time that night, I *sang*. As the melody poured out of my mouth, rivers of living water flooded my heart. I felt all brand new, a childlike hope eclipsing my doubt. Surrender had accomplished its goal, and I belted out a fresh anthem of freedom.

CHOOSING TO SING

Beloved, it's time to sing your song.

When it's all you can do to pull yourself out of bed and make it through your day, choosing to sing in the middle of your desert can feel like an impossibility.

But it's an undeniable truth of the Kingdom: your song of praise acts as a holy sacrifice, powerfully paving the way for breakthrough. It shatters demonic strongholds and routs the forces of evil. It elevates your perspective and provides a conduit for supernatural faith. It acts as an angelic commission, calling Heaven to move on your behalf.

Hosea 2:15 explains that our desert song is a *response*. It's how we react to the demonstration of Jesus' heart as He leads us through the wilderness.

Longing, adoration, captivation.

Joy, praise, thanksgiving.

I am called to give my offering of response to God *before* I leave the barrenness of the wilderness, not once I finally occupy my promised land. When I yield my spirit to the overcoming power of the Holy Spirit, His strength becomes mine. His song becomes my own. In the light of eternity, the One who sees the beginning from the end knows that my breakthrough is poised just around the corner. As I partner my heart with heaven's reality, I step into that supernatural stream and a melody bursts forth.

In those moments when I don't feel capable of singing, *I have to choose.* Like David, I have to push past my despair and impending sense of defeat and command my soul to praise. I can't allow my circumstances to dictate my choice, trapping me in inaction.

Solomon sagely describes it this way, *"If you faint in the day of adversity, your strength is small"* (Proverbs 24:10).

Dear one, don't faint.

Instead, strengthen yourself in the Lord (*1 Samuel 30:6*). Let your heart delight in His great goodness and covenantal loyalty. Gaze deep into His eyes and discover afresh His deeply satisfying love.

Then, speak to your soul and command it to bless the Lord.

> *"Bless the Lord, O my soul, and all that is within me, bless His holy name!"*
> Psalm 103:1

MY LOVE SONG

As I was in the process of writing this chapter, I experienced first-hand the power of singing into the breakthrough. One of my precious granddaughters suffers from cerebral palsy, a condition which was discovered when she was just a few months old. Our family was devastated by the diagnosis, and my daughter and son-in-law reeled to find a place of solid emotional footing in the wake of the news.

In the two years since that announcement, our entire family has banded together for multiple days of prayer and fasting, believing by faith that God is mighty to heal our precious one. As of this writing, that healing has yet to be fully released.

Often over the course of the past two years, the Holy Spirit has led me into times of bold intercessory declaration for our granddaughter. He has prompted me to praise Him for her healing, even as she has fallen further behind in her development. He has asked me to bless Him for His goodness over her life right in the moments of my deepest grief and discouragement. And most often, He has prompted me to sing. To worship Him with abandon when my heart was heavy with pain, trusting that He alone can see the end of her story.

It's been a deeply sacrificial song of praise.

While I was driving to a friend's home in central California for a brief writing retreat, a text came through my phone. It was a video of my granddaughter, and she was crawling. Stiff and new, like a baby colt just dropped from its momma's womb, her legs and arms were jerkily propelling her across the floor.

It was a moment for which we had been praying, declaring, and believing, hoping against hope. And in the tight space of my car, right in the middle of LA freeway congestion, I exploded with laughter, tears, and song. For 45 minutes, the praise erupted from my soul. *You are always and forever faithful, Jesus!*

He is so faithful. Right in the middle of your desert season, He is always deeply faithful. And because He is faithful, He is worthy of your song of lavish love.

> *"Sing to God, sing praises to his name; lift up a song to him who rides through the deserts; his name is the Lord; exult before him! Father of the fatherless and protector of the widows is God in his holy habitation. God settles the solitary in a home; he leads out the prisoners to prosperity, but the rebellious dwell in a parched land."*
> Psalm 68:4-6

No trouble can overcome My plans for your life, beloved. No pain can push away My purpose. Respond to me as you did when you first tasted My love. Give

Me your whole heart without reservation. How I long to take you in My arms and gather you under My wings! Don't resist My deep chesed, My steadfast love.

Only I can orchestrate all things so that every stumbling block which the enemy has put into your path, intending to cause you harm, can turn to great good and defeat his every scheme. You will no longer be defined by trouble.

Although My love and My ways are so spectacular that they are past finding out, I have come to live with you, to make My home with you. Together let's build a home for your heart on the immovable rock of truth. When you build with Me, you will never be shaken.

Let your song come out. Let your praise rise. Your melody of complete abandon is a call to My heart which I will never resist.

---

1. Michel Hendricks and Jim Wilder. *The Other Half of Church* (Chicago: Moody Publishers, 2020), pp. 13-73.

SEVEN

lean on your beloved

> "Who is that coming up out of the wilderness, leaning on her beloved?"
> Song of Solomon 8:5

> "And I will betroth you to me forever. I will betroth you to me in righteousness and in justice, in steadfast love and in mercy. I will betroth you to me in faithfulness. And you shall know the Lord."
> Hosea 2:19-20

I LOVE TO HIKE.

I relish experiencing God's creation in outdoor spaces, the tangy air filling my lungs, and fresh views stretching in every direction. I love the push—the way I have to challenge my body through the tough spots. And I love the clean rush of endorphins when I make it to the other side of the climb.

Whenever my family camps or travels to a new place, I anticipate discovering a new trail. Familiar hikes are favorites; I know what to expect around each bend and how much time is required to complete the route. But an untried walk is an adventure. Each turn in the path opens a new vista, a view I've never before experienced. I'm not certain how long the trail will take, but I'm fine with that. The unknown nature of the journey is half of its charm. And when I round that final bend and realize I've reached my destination, it feels delightfully unexpected.

Just as with each earthly trail that we travel, our wasteland journeys will carry us to the moment in which we realize that we have reached our destination.

Jesus is calling us out of the desert.

UP FROM THE WILDERNESS

At some point in my own story, I stumbled across Song of Songs 8:5 like I had never seen it before. And I was mesmerized by the truth which it so powerfully portrays.

> *"Who is that coming up out of the wilderness, leaning on her beloved?"*

With those words, I was caught by a vision of the bride which stunned me with its beauty.

The King hasn't led His beloved into the wilderness indefinitely. At just the right moment, they round a bend in the trail, and she spots a view of the path ahead leading up from the desert floor. Before her are fertile fields shining in the sunlight. The sound of rushing water fills her ears as springs bubble from the hillsides. The scent of honey blossoms perfumes the air, rich and sweet. Her breath catches with the realization that, even as she climbs, the desert is transitioning to the lush green of fruitfulness. Overcome by joy, she turns for a final glimpse behind her. The muted shades of scrub and sand blend to create a backdrop which no longer feels threatening, but instead holds the remembrance of monument moments with her King. With a rush of deepest love and gratitude, the bride threads her arm through her Beloved's. Exhaling, she leans her head against His chest, and together they climb the path into promise.

The Father has not abandoned you to the heat of the desert. He has never intended to leave you there, wandering and waiting for a promise which never arrives. His singular focus has been to lead you out, your head resting against the heart of your King. His purpose has always been to do you good—to use affliction and suffering to tune your ears to the nuances of His voice so that He can lavish you with abundance.

A BROAD PLACE

I love how Elihu, the only comforter who God didn't rebuke for misrepresenting His heart and character to Job, describes the purpose of our suffering seasons:

> *"He delivers the afflicted by their affliction and opens their ear by adversity. He also allured you out of distress into a broad place where there was no cramping, and what was set on your table was full of fatness"*
> Job 36:15-16

The Living Bible renders verse 15 in this way, *"But by means of their suffering, he rescues those who suffer. For he gets their attention through adversity."*

Elihu expresses a profound understanding that the very tool which the Father uses to deliver His afflicted ones is *affliction*. In other words, our hardships, trials, and challenges are the catalysts for a transformation that rescues us from the strongholds and torment of the enemy. They also deliver us from ourselves: our fleshly attitudes, responses, and perspectives that keep us in opposition to the truth of God.

Elihu also explains that God's objective is for our closed ears to be opened during tough times. As we lean into His heart, the Lord sharpens our hearing. Instead of being hindered by stubborn defiance or rebellious pride, our wilderness is designed to bring us to a place of clarity, understanding, and response to the voice of Jesus.

All of that truth is so rich; however, my favorite part of Elihu's speech is verse 16:

> *"He also allured you out of distress into a broad place where there was no cramping, and what was set on your table was full of fatness."*

Although he uses a different Hebrew word than the one which Hosea employs to describe how God draws me to Himself, Elihu's core meaning is the same. God allures me. He calls me out of distress, and when I respond, He leads me to the place which He has prepared for me. It's a broad place, a wide place where I can stretch out and thrive. It's a place where He has prepared a table specifically for me that's loaded with the most delicious of delicacies.

Elihu's description calls to mind David's words from Psalm 18:31-36.

> *"For who is God, but the Lord? And who is a rock, except our God?—the God who equipped me with strength and made my way blameless. He made my feet like the feet of a deer and set me secure on the heights. He trains my hands for war, so that my arms can bend a bow of bronze. You have given me the shield of your salvation, and your right hand supported me, and your gentleness made me great. You gave a wide place for my steps under me, and my feet did not slip."*

This is the heart of your Father. To lead you up from the desert to a broad place. But before He can take you there, you have to allow the wilderness to accomplish its purpose in your life.

PARTNERING WITH HIS WORD

Hundreds of years before John the Baptist hit Israel's national scene, the prophet Isaiah recorded the words of the Lord which describe John's future mission:

> *"A voice cries: 'In the wilderness prepare the way of the Lord; make straight in the desert a highway for our God. Every valley shall be lifted up, and every mountain and hill be made low; the uneven ground shall become level, and the rough places a plain. And the glory of the Lord shall be revealed, and all flesh*

> *shall see it together, for the mouth of the Lord has spoken.'"*
> Isaiah 40:3-5

Although this passage is specific to the Baptizer's life, it also provides keen insight into the purpose of our own desert stints. While John lived in the physical wilderness of Judea, calling Israel to repentance and making her ready for the advent of the Messiah, Isaiah's description has a crucial application for our own lives.

The path of God is prepared in our wasteland.

Our seasons of favor and abundance can only accomplish part of what is needed to pave the way for our souls to experience His fullness. Jesus allures us into that dry place so that we can begin the process of making a straight highway for our God. By the power of grace, we partner with the Spirit in clearing our soul's rubble, making a smooth road for Him to travel in our lives. Stumbling blocks are removed and pitfalls are filled. It's a straight highway that we're building, one without obstacles which hinder His work in and through us.

Isaiah also declares that every valley is to be lifted up and every mountain to be brought low. This indicates a divine partnership between ourselves and the Holy Spirit.

Remember Jesus' words to His disciples from Mark 11:23?

> *"Truly, I say to you, whoever says to this mountain, 'Be taken up and thrown into the sea,' and does not doubt in his heart, but believes that what he says will come to pass, it will be done for him."*

When the Lord's path in my life is hindered by a mountain, I have a choice. I can either endlessly circle that obstacle, hoping at some point that I'll be lucky enough to find a way around it. Or I can choose faith and speak to it.

Move.

In the same way, I partner with the Spirit to command every low place.

Be raised.

These hindrances force me to confront what's hidden in my heart. When I'm confronted with my mountain and valley impossibilities, do I play the part of the victim? Do I languish in self-pity or stomp around in resentment? Or do I choose to believe the words of my Savior and declare, *"Prepare the way of the Lord!"*

A HIGHWAY IN YOUR HEART

I'm a history buff. Having lived most of my adult life in Southern California, I'm constantly reminded of the Spanish men and women who pioneered the western part of our nation. Surrounded by the remnants of that long-ago culture, I'm especially aware of their legacy when traveling our streets. The greater part of California roads have Spanish names, a fact which allows tourists to be easily spotted and teased behind their sunburned backs due to their hopeless mispronunciations.

Over the years, I've settled on my favorite local street name, *El Camino Real*, translated in English as *The King's Highway*. Running almost the entire length of the California coastline, the trail which became known as *El Camino Real* was blazed to carry Spanish soldiers and missionaries as they spread their homeland's governance and faith throughout California.

Father Junipero Serra, one of my missionary heroes, traveled *El Camino Real* as he pioneered missions across the frontier for the purpose of sharing the gospel of Jesus with the indigenous peoples. Most of those missions can still be visited today, preserved reminders of one Franciscan friar's determination to pave the way for the glory of God in the wilderness.

The result of all of this clearing out and raising up

should be obvious: it's all for His glory. Once the path has been prepared, I can lift my head and realize that although I may have been long in the construction process, my heart has been cemented with my own personal *El Camino Real*, a highway upon which His glory can be displayed in my life. And when it is, *"all flesh shall see it together."* Those around me will recognize the majesty and beauty of the King. His name will be magnified through me, and the world will be impacted. And the most exciting part is that it doesn't end with me. My *yes* to the paving process leaves a legacy for future generations. Years from now, the heavenly mile markers in my life will help to guide the path of those who will follow in my spiritual footsteps.

BELOVED HUSBAND

As we round the final bend in our journey together, I want us to grab hold of one last nugget from Hosea's story. From verse 15 through to its end, chapter 2 is chock-full of the extraordinary results of Israel's wilderness wooing.

Let's examine verses 16-17:

> *"And in that day, declares the Lord, you will call me 'My Husband' and no longer will you call me 'My Baal'. For I will remove the names of the Baals from*

her mouth, and they shall be remembered by name no more."

The Lord is promising Israel that on the other side of their wilderness, they will walk in a relationship with Him on a completely different level. Their restored dynamic will be so heart-revolutionary that they will be compelled to call God by a new name. It's a name which He Himself has consistently used, but due to their lack of intimacy, pain, fear, and sin, they haven't yet embraced it.

The word *Baal* is used throughout the Old Testament to reference a specific demonic entity, an idol worshiped by the Canaanites. However, in this verse, the Hebrew word which Hosea chooses is *Baali*, which means *My Master;* this is the only instance in the entire Old Testament in which this word is used. Through Hosea's words, the Lord is explaining that Israel's desert sojourn will not only transform their own identity from that of a slave to a lover, but it will also change their understanding of God, shifting their view of Him from master to husband.

In our current culture, relating to the idea of a "master" can be challenging. Starting with the abolishing of slavery in the mid-1800s and continuing with the women's rights movement throughout the 1900s, women have moved towards unprecedented social freedom. This dynamic has rendered the term "master" obsolete on most levels. However, if we backtrack just 200 years, we can remember the hundreds of thousands of women who never had the opportunity to experience the love and tenderness of a faithful husband. Instead, they lived under the rule of slave owners who viewed them as mere property, acquired solely for their gain. If we travel back four thousand years further, we encounter the Jewish nation enslaved for 400 years by the Egyptians. Forced to toil merely to sustain themselves and their children, the Israelites endured harsh living conditions and even harsher treatment.

After God led the Jews out from the bondage of Egypt, Israel had to learn how to live as a nation of freed individuals. Yet, without the transformational power of the Holy Spirit, breaking free from their slavery mindset proved nearly impossible. So when Moses took a little too long on Mt. Sinai while receiving the Old Covenant, impatient Israel reverted to their idols, effectively returning to spiritual slavery. This thread of servitude persisted through their collective identity, extending to Hosea's era. Consequently, few Jews were able to perceive God as anything other than a master: a stern and demanding God, bearing far too many similarities to the Canaanite god Baal.

But Jesus is relentless in *The Pursuit* of the hearts of His people. His goal is to transform our mindsets so completely that we no longer relate to Him as master. Instead, we embrace Him as our beloved Husband—the only One who has the right and privilege to protect and guide us, bringing us up and out of our desert places.

WILDERNESS TRANSFORMATION

I believe the patriarch Joseph powerfully models for us what it looks like to come up from the wilderness leaning on our Beloved. After sharing his supernatural dreams of imminent leadership with his family, Joseph is sold by his jealous brothers into Egyptian slavery, experiencing an intensely challenging desert season. Unjustly accused and imprisoned, then forgotten and abandoned, Joseph's heart is tested deeply by the Lord. Because his wilderness was preparation for his promotion, it was the posture of his heart which most concerned the Father.

Psalm 105:16-22 paints a powerful picture of Joseph's journey:

> *"And He (the Lord) called for a famine upon the land (Egypt); He broke the whole staff of bread. He sent a man before them, Joseph, who was sold as a slave. They afflicted his feet with fetters, he himself was laid in irons; until the time that his word came to pass, the word of the LORD tested him. The king sent and released him, the ruler of*

> *peoples, and set him free. He made him lord of his house and ruler over all his possessions, to imprison his princes at will, that he might teach his elders wisdom."*

The Psalmist explains that the *rhema* (uttered or spoken) word of the Lord which came to Joseph in the form of prophetic dreams was the very thing which God uses to profoundly test him. Joseph is confident that God has spoken to him. He is so convinced of that message that as a youth, he presumptuously shares his dreams with his entire family, fanning into flame the hatred of his brothers. As a result, for years Joseph's heart is tested by the seeming unfulfillment of that prophetic word.

But throughout the pain and pressure, the word of the Lord continues to speak to his spirit, challenging him to hope. Calling him to believe in faith as every circumstance taunts him otherwise. Reminding him to remain steadfast in his integrity, clinging to righteousness in the face of discouragement and temptation.

When Joseph least expects it, his *suddenly* moment arrives. Called before Pharaoh to interpret the ruler's troubling prophetic dreams, Joseph is catapulted from infamy into a place of authority and influence, second only to Egypt's king. As he responds to Pharaoh's request, he reveals the priceless result of his wilderness transformation, stating, *"It is not in me. God will give Pharoah a favorable answer"* (*Genesis 41:16*).

The once highly favored son of his earthly father, who as a youth brashly declared his God-given destiny, now stands as the tested and humbled favored son of his heavenly Father. As he leans on the arm of his Beloved, Joseph walks into his long-held promise, completely dependent on the One who has brought him out shining as pure gold.

POSTURE OF INTIMACY

Due to his powerful prophetic experiences and undeniable heart transformation, Joseph will always be one of my favorite Old Testament heroes. But when it comes to New Testament characters, John is undeniably my top choice. Just one perusal of his five canonized books alerts you to the fact that both his perspective of the gospel and his relationship with Jesus is unique. His language is Kingdom prose, a beautiful demonstration that the Good News is never solely about the mere facts of the story. John's focus is always the heart of Jesus which he weaves masterfully into every line.

John was a lover.

In spite of the reality that he was also a rough-and-ready fisherman and a risk-taking pioneer, John knew what it meant to embrace deep intimacy with the Lord.

This understanding saturates every phrase which he employs in his writings, as exemplified in his Spirit-birthed epithet for the Church: *Beloved.*

While some theologians belittle John for his self-chosen moniker of *the disciple whom Jesus loved*, I believe it's a powerful window into the transformation of his identity. When Jesus calls John from his life along Galilee's shores to follow after Him, John's focus shifts from daily survival to releasing the power of the Kingdom of God on earth. But this change is entirely rooted in the person of Jesus. Who Jesus is—how He lives, speaks, thinks and acts—becomes the core of John's world. He lives to know Him. To be loved by Him and to love Him. Nowhere is this demonstrated as beautifully as in John 13:21-26:

> *"After saying these things, Jesus was troubled in his spirit, and testified, 'Truly, truly, I say to you, one of you will betray me.' The disciples looked at one another, uncertain of whom he spoke. One of his disciples, whom Jesus loved, was reclining at table at Jesus' side, so Simon Peter motioned to him to ask Jesus of whom he was speaking. So that disciple, leaning back against Jesus, said to him, 'Lord, who is it?' Jesus answered, 'It is he to whom I will give this morsel of bread when I have dipped it.' So when he had dipped the morsel, he gave it to Judas, the son of Simon Iscariot."*

While the context of this story is important to the overall Gospel narrative, I want to focus on the simple fact that *"one of his disciples, whom Jesus loved, was reclining at table at Jesus' side."*

As thirteen men gather around this Passover meal, one of the twelve disciples partaking with Jesus is a traitor. And of the eleven remaining faithful, only one is close enough to Jesus to lean against His side.

The original rendering of this phrase in the Greek gives us a fuller understanding of John's posture. The word *kólpos* indicates *"properly, the upper part of the chest where a garment naturally folded to form a 'pocket'—called the 'bosom,' the position synonymous with intimacy (union)"*. John is reclining in the bosom of Jesus. In other words, he is in a position of closest intimacy, leaning against His heart.

This is the posture which propelled John through the disillusionment of Christ's crucifixion, the exhilaration of His resurrection, and the transformation of Pentecost. It's what allowed him to lead apostolically and father the early Church through its establishment, persecution, and dispersion. It's what carried him through losing his closest friends to Rome's arenas, supported him through several martyrdom attempts, and strengthened him during his isolated exile on Patmos. John knew what it meant to lean on the chest of his

Beloved. He knew how to position himself to listen to Jesus' heartbeat—to carry His secrets, understanding His joys and His pain.

LEAN ON YOUR BELOVED

And in this, we find the crux of the wilderness message.

Lean, dear one.

Through all of your dusty wanderings, your precipice climbs, and your sojourns in the valley of the shadow, you have been called to this primary posture.

Lean on your Beloved.

This is the position of the woman who has journeyed deep with Jesus. Rather than grabbing hold of the world's blaring message to come out of her wilderness standing straighter, head held higher, she *leans*. And in that position, every secret place, every tried place of her heart is expressed in a single gesture: here is a woman who has embraced The Pursuit.

As a Kingdom daughter and lover of Jesus, I pray that you will be marked as a woman who *joyfully leans*—one who reclines on His chest, catching the nuance of every heartbeat as it pulses with holy passion just for you.

I pray that you will be one who allows yourself to be truly seen and fully known by the Lover of your soul.

And as He leads you up from your wilderness, I pray that your heart will join with the declaration of that heavenly chorus of witnesses:

> "This is my Beloved and this is my friend, O daughters of Jerusalem!
> I am my Beloved's and His desire is for me.
> His banner over me is love."
> Song of Solomon 5:16b, 7:10 & 2:4b

I am your Husband, beloved. With Me, you are safe. I am your protector, deliverer, and provider. I deliver you from sickness, from disease. I bring you out from the roaring waters that threaten to overwhelm you, and I plant your feet upon a rock.

Do not allow lack to define you. I have broken the curse of lack through My shed blood, and now you inherit every spiritual blessing in the heavenly places. You will not only overcome every obstacle in your path but also be more than a conqueror through My Spirit.

Allow My Spirit to fill you freshly every moment. To truly live, you need My Spirit just as you need the air in your lungs. My power will propel you beyond your fears. Lean into My embrace and rest your weary head on My heart. You will find rest for your soul as you yoke yourself to Me, learning from My humble instruction.

Tenderly, I will lead you up from the wilderness and place you into the promises I have reserved just for you. Your land of covenant may be populated by giants, but together we will defeat each one. Only believe.

My beautiful one, I am fully yours just as you are Mine.

about the author

With a pastoral legacy that reaches back four generations, Tiffany has discipled, counseled, mentored, and taught women of all ages for over 30 years. She is cofounder of three organizations: CANOPI, an international equipping ministry based in Central America, NewSong, an international collective of micro-churches, and The Prophetic Collective, a ministry which equips women to walk in their spiritual gifts. Although she enjoys teaching, Tiffany thrives most when introducing women to scriptural truths about their identity in Christ. Visit www.streamroots.com for more information.

facebook.com/streamroots
instagram.com/streamroots
bookbub.com/authors/tiffany-nesbitt
amazon.com/author/tiffanynesbitt

also by tiffany nesbitt

Bless Bible Study

Into the Wilderness Bible Study

Made in the USA
Las Vegas, NV
20 March 2024